REVIVAL IN

Revival in Manchester 1859-74

The Thrilling, Untold Story

PAUL MOULD

ISBN: 9798768944087

Bible Quotations:

DEDICATION

In Memory of Henry Moorhouse (1840-80)

"For God so loved the world that He gave His only begotten Son, that whoever believes in Him should not perish but have everlasting life."

John 3:16 (NKJV)

ACKNOWLEDGMENTS

My sincere thanks go Michael Marcel and Geoff Green for permission to freely use material from their web pages on revivals in the UK. Thanks especially to my wife for encouraging me to start this project, for your support, patience and proof-reading.

PREFACE

I think it was around 2015 when I heard a church leader say that someone had told him "There has never been a revival in Manchester". I was somewhat taken aback by this comment, finding it difficult to believe that on no occasion in history had there been a revival in Manchester. At that time, however, I had never read anything that had informed me to the contrary. There is certainly no coherent account that has previously been published on the subject. And so I set about the task to discover whether there ever had been a revival in Manchester.

The material I have used to write this book has come almost entirely from on-line resources, freely available on the world-wide web. I want to make it clear at the outset that I have frequently quoted my sources almost verbatim, and only changed a few words, or the punctuation, to make the sense clearer. I have also on occasion had to modernise the English (please also see the Glossary). I have sometimes also inserted words in [square brackets] to explain the meaning more fully. Hence, this book is much more of a compilation of reports than a retelling in my own words the story of the Revival in Manchester. I am especially indebted to the web sites of Geoff Green (https://www.liverpoolrevival.org.uk and www.1859.org.uk) and Michael Marcel (ukwells.org). Both of these authors have graciously given me permission to freely use their material. I have endeavoured to cite my sources as much as possible; I apologise in advance for any omissions. It should also be pointed out that I have, in almost all cases, used the anglicised spelling of words for the benefit of UK readers.

The outcome of my research is to show that Manchester has indeed had a revival, and probably at least two revivals (1859-62 and 1874). This conclusion is not mine alone, it is the conclusion of revival historians and, most importantly, the verdict of those who lived through that period and described it in their own words. Moreover, as the story progresses, the reader will discover that not only has Manchester had a revival, it has also been the source of revival to other places and countries (especially through the life of Ardwick-born evangelist Henry Moorhouse).

It is my hope that the reader will be deeply moved by this thrilling, largely untold story. May it bring a new confidence in the gospel message – "the power of God for the salvation of everyone who believes" (Romans 1:16, BSB). History tells us that revivals often start when people read about past revivals.

If ever Manchester (and the UK) needed another revival, it is now. Our earnest prayer should be "Do it again, Lord!" and "Send a revival, and let it begin with me!".

Paul Mould, Manchester, England, 2021

GLOSSARY

Alhambra: A building (e.g. theatre) with similar architecture to the Alhambra palace in Granada, Spain.
(The) anxious: persons deeply concerned about their spiritual condition.
Collier: coal miner.
Crowded to excess: overcrowded.
Impenitent: those who refuse to repent (of their sin).
Infidel: an unbeliever, especially one strongly opposed to the gospel message.
Inquirers: those asking "What must I do to be saved?".
Inquiry-room: A room set aside where inquirers could go after the main meeting.
Nonjurors: Church of England congregations that refused to swear allegiance to William III (William of Orange).
Nonconformist: Protestant churches that were separate from the Church of England.
Passeth by: passes by.
Provinces: areas of England outside of London.
Romanists: Roman Catholics.
Supplicant: someone deep in prayer.
Sabbath (or Lord's day): Sunday.
Thee/Thou: you.
Thy: your.

CONTENTS

1 INTRODUCTION

The City of Manchester

Manchester first expanded at the start of the Industrial Revolution. From a small town – actually a village with no town council – of less than 10 000 inhabitants in the early 1700s, it rose by the 1860s to a bustling city of a third of a million! The populous ran the whole spectrum from those who came and made their fortunes to some of the poorest in terms of housing, exploitation and squalor in the whole country. [1]

During the first half of the eighteenth century Manchester was already becoming a marketing and organizing centre for the emerging cotton industry. The known denominations present in the early decades were the Anglicans, Nonjurors, Presbyterians, Baptists, Quakers and Roman Catholics. All but the Anglicans and Presbyterians were as yet generally insignificant in numbers and influence. [2]

The evangelical revival in the period 1740-1800 appears to have made only a relatively small impact on the Manchester population during this period, with the Methodists themselves only boasting a membership of a little over 2200 in 1799, despite many visits to the area by the Wesley brothers. [3] Nonetheless, a foundation of evangelical churches was laid in the city, ready for the years of harvest that lay ahead.

The neighbouring city of Liverpool gave rise to many great evangelists in the mid-1800s. These included: Reginald Radcliffe, Canon Hay Aitken, John Hambleton, John Latham and Edward Usher. Many of these preachers would spend a good deal of time in Manchester and the surrounding towns during the 1859 revival and the years following. Mention should also be made of the great American evangelist James Caughey, who led a revival in Liverpool in the early 1840s; he returned to England in 1860 with powerful effect. [4]

The world's first inter-city railway opened in 1830, making transport between the two cities cheap and easy. Co-incidentally, the railway also enabled revival blessing to be readily transported from one city to the other. Reginald Radcliffe commented: "Between Liverpool and Manchester there lies a great bog [known as Chat Moss], and before George Stephenson could connect these two towns he had to overcome this enormous difficulty...The workmen obeyed his directions; and now it is so easy to run to and fro between these towns that it does not occur to a passenger that there was ever any extraordinary difficulty. Crowds of human beings and thousands of tons of heavy goods pass merrily to and fro by day and even by night." [5]

Hence, the two cities became strongly linked, not only in commerce but also in revival.

The work of the evangelists often aroused great

opposition and persecution in the early 1850s as the following report (from 1854) shows:

Their first stand was in Stephenson's Square [in Manchester] where they encountered opposition hitherto not experienced. [The people's] very faces quivered with rage; loud yells of men, women and children pierced the air, so that it seemed as if Satan's kingdom trembled at these two men preaching the simple gospel. The terrible noise drowned out their voices, but they continued with their witness and a poor man's heart was touched by their testimony. They were then directed to take their stand at a lamp between the old cathedral church and a notorious singing saloon. They determined not to give up the spot until dragged from it. One night a man arrived leading a gang of ruffians with all the rage and malice it was possible to conceive. They both scoffed and beat them and whilst this was happening a total stranger rushed between them taking hold of both their arms and said, "Brethren, let us pray". While they were praying, however, the leader of the group put his hand on Hambleton's mouth, went on mocking still, and they were carried by the crowd from the spot by force. Walking through the streets, hundreds following them like dogs, biting into bits the tracts they had given out, jumping on the bits, which they had spat from their mouths...God, however, delivered them, and they returned yet again to the lamppost that they felt that God had given them. In the years that followed people came to Christ in that very spot, and other preachers were raised up to continue the work there. Their pioneering work around lanes, streets, and the lampposts of Manchester were well rewarded in the years that followed."[6]

In only a few short years the atmosphere was to change dramatically.

What is Revival?

Revival is not the same as an evangelistic campaign, although revival can break forth out of such an event. "The distinguishing features, which separate revival from a successful evangelistic campaign are: weeping over sin, people being broken before the Lord..., confession of sin..., requests for forgiveness, reconciliations, restitutions and reparation where necessary". "Revival first of all touches and renews the church. In turn, this renewal leads to a spiritual awakening, where many people are saved and communities transformed." [7] During times of revival there is a supernatural acceleration of God's work, bringing a harvest of souls in one year that might take ten years or more of regular church evangelism. "In times of evangelism, the evangelist seeks the sinner; in times of revival the sinner comes chasing after the Lord" [8]. Where before there was hostility, now there is a great openness to the gospel message. The evangelists could testify: "our gospel came to you not only in word, but also in power, in the Holy Spirit, and with great conviction." (1 Thessalonians 1:5 BSB). Conversions tended to be deep and lasting.

Critics may often put revivals down to 'religious enthusiasm' but during the nineteenth century fervent outward displays of emotion tended to be frowned upon, while the work was thought to be more blessed if it was carried out in a solemn and dignified manner (especially in England).

Only the Holy Spirit can bring about true revival. So it was that in 1859 a fresh breeze was blowing over the land.

Revival hits the UK

"The 1859 Revival was one that affected virtually the whole of the UK, and in terms of the actual numbers converted was probably the greatest revival we have ever had in this country. The amazing thing is that whilst most people will be fully aware of the Methodist Revival [ca. 1740-1800], the 1904 Welsh Revival, and the 1949 Hebrides Revival, very few people will be even aware that there was such a revival in this country at that time. I think that it is sometimes referred to as 'the forgotten revival'. It is also sometimes referred to as 'the layman's revival' [because the main evangelists were not ordained clergy and had ordinary jobs]." [9]

The revival was very much a revival amongst the ordinary people, especially the poor. A number of the great evangelists were, in fact, drawn from the ranks of the vilest characters in society; thereby illustrating the eternal truth that God uses the foolish things of the world to shame the wise, and the weak things of this world to shame the strong (1 Corinthians 1:27). The conversion and transformation of 'the worst of sinners' often created something of a sensation, attracting many people to see and hear them.

Manchester and Liverpool were thought to be very difficult places to reach with the gospel, but both cities saw a tremendous move of the Spirit at this time. Radcliffe commented "If Liverpool and Manchester…why not every city, town, and village in the world?". [10]

2 THE 1859 REVIVAL: AN OVERVIEW

Revival begins in New York

In July 1857, a young evangelist named Jeremiah Lanphier started a weekly prayer meeting for businessmen in central New York. Only six attended the first meeting, but the attendance grew to 10,000 by the close of the year. This was the humble beginnings of a mighty move of God, which in the following two years added at least a million people to the membership of the American churches.

Revival reaches the UK

The revival wave crossed the Atlantic in 1859, reaching Ireland first of all. In Ulster (Northern Ireland) there was a remarkable time of ingathering, with 100,000 added to Protestant churches in the calendar year. Subsequently, there were great revivals in both Scotland and Wales, with 300,000 and 100,000, respectively, added to the churches in those nations (about 10% of the entire population). The work in England got off to a slower start.

"The work in Ulster, Wales and Scotland, was somewhat different in character to that of most of England. In the former the revival was more spontaneous, and most of the conversions occurred during the year of

1859. In England, however, the initial move was not quite as dramatic as in the [other] parts of the country, but within two years something else happened which resulted in large numbers of people coming to Christ: God raised up a large number of evangelists who travelled the length and breadth of the land preaching the gospel, and many thousands of people were brought into the kingdom by this means. By 1864 no less than 600,000 people were converted in England, bringing the total in the UK to over one million people. Even parts of Southern Ireland [mainly Roman Catholic] were affected by the revival, including the capital, Dublin…" [11]

"The start of the revival in England is much more difficult to relate as there does not seem to be a clear story here. The other three countries have a very clear beginning but England doesn't, and the reason for this is that virtually nobody seems to have written [a proper account] about the revival in this nation. Apart from Edwin Orr's book, "The Second Evangelical Awakening" written in 1949 [12], [there has been very little] written on the subject. Orr's main source was 'The Revival' [also referred to as 'Revival Newspaper'] weekly newspaper that started in July 1859 in order to record the revival in the UK. It was wonderful, as far as it went, but on its own admission, due to its size of 8 pages, it did not have the room to publish all the revival accounts it was sent, and then of course there were all the stories that were never sent to them.

A sign of what was coming [in England] took place in Hayle, Cornwall through the ministry of William Haslam. There was a revival in his church from 1857 until he left in 1860. The first united prayer meetings I have read about were in Newcastle in September 1858, and then in Scarborough in July 1859. In August a revival went on in the Staffordshire collieries, 500 being saved in one place, and a big revival seems to have started in Newcastle in October, with 1,300 being saved in one month, just in one church. Revivals broke out here and there towards the end of 1859, particularly in about four Primitive Methodist Circuits. Most of the local revivals were ignited by regular prayer or by testimony about what was going on in America or Ulster. The light that seemed to start the fire - particularly in London - was the worldwide prayer meeting that took place in the whole second week of 1860.

'The Revival' newspaper gave about a half of its space for reporting on the revival in England, to London. This is not really surprising considering it had 2.8 million people, which was nearly seven times as big as the two next biggest cities of Glasgow and Liverpool [around 400,000 each]. Although there are many accounts of revival in England I do not get the feeling of the [whole] country being on fire, as I do with the other three countries.

One pastor explains the beginning of a revival - "Indications of revival were observed in the quiet stillness which pervaded the congregation, in the earnest desire and deep anxiety of the members to see among them a general awakening, in the extraordinary spirit of prayer which was poured out upon the people and their faith in the efficacy of prayer, and in some mysterious influence, almost irresistible, which I felt upon my own mind, by which, for some time before. I was all but impelled to preach to my people from certain subjects preparatory to the coming blessing."

Prayer was the key to the revival in England as well as the other home countries and many children were involved. - "They cannot but pray; they are filled with the spirit of prayer, and consequently they pray with an unction and a readiness, and frequency, and earnestness, which must strike with astonishment all who hear them"

As in other parts of the UK, people started united prayer meetings on hearing the revival news from different areas. In London daily meetings were organised in Crosby Hall in September 1859 and by the end of the year there were 120 prayer meetings in the city, a quarter of them daily, the rest weekly. The numbers grew until it was better to ask where [there wasn't] a prayer meeting. The movement was unprecedented. After a year there were less large prayer meetings - probably because people were out there doing stuff [evangelising].

Unlike anywhere else, people got together to plan how to reach the vast numbers in London. One of the most successful ideas was to hire theatres and halls to hold meetings for the workers and the poor during the winter season, people who generally had never set foot in a church before. This was only possible because the Earl of Shaftesbury had promoted a bill four years earlier that allowed Christian meetings in un-consecrated buildings. At the beginning of 1860 he formed a committee and by the end of February they hired seven theatres where 20k people heard the gospel every Sunday. For the upper and middle classes, St Paul's, [Westminster] Abbey and two halls were hired in the West End. Seeing how successful these meetings were, others hired halls and theatres across London, until there were about 20 venues being hired, and an estimated one million people heard the gospel each season.

Generally speaking these Sunday services were led by itinerant revivalists such as the amazing Reginald Radcliffe and Richard Weaver. Wherever they went the venues could not hold the numbers who wanted to get in and many gave their lives to Jesus in each service. Although testimonies were often given during the services, they were dominated by preaching.

As well as these large general meetings there were initiatives all over the capital to reach different groups... People held meetings in schools, hospitals, parks, factories and orphanages – just about anywhere where there were unsaved people.

It is not known how many were saved in London, but clearly a great proportion were reached with the gospel. One person wrote, "There must be a great deal of good doing in London, for one can hardly pass the end of a street of a fine evening or of a Sunday, without hearing someone preaching, and not only men but women".

The revival in London seems to have been pretty powerful through the whole of 1860 and 1861. At the end of 1861 Reginald Radcliffe wrote – 'as regards the present movement, [it is] far ahead of our large provincial towns. There is no one to take the lead [in those towns] as here. I have never seen any part of Scotland or Ireland more ripe for blessings than many parts of England are now. The Holy Ghost has been moving over thousands, convincing them of sins, and now they want to be gathered in."' [13]

"In 1859-60, the work of God was making progress in

various cities and towns of Lancashire. Labourers whom the Lord of the harvest had thrust into the field were reaping in plenty. The time was full of energy, hope, and joy. Great meetings were held in Manchester, where thousands, assembled in the Circus, in the Alhambra [Portland Street], and other places of meeting, were addressed by such well-known men as Wilbraham Taylor, Robert Baxter, Stevenson Blackwood, W. R Lockhart, Reginald Radcliffe, Richard Weaver, Alfred Trench, Lord Radstock, and many more." [14]

Manchester and Liverpool became heavily involved in the revival, but not until a little later than London. Liverpool had a population slightly larger than Manchester at that time (about 400,000 versus 350,000).

"Charles Finney, the American revivalist had good meetings in Manchester in July 1860 and James Caughey in Liverpool a couple of months earlier, but it appears that both cities did not really get going until autumn 1861. At that time Radcliffe and Weaver, plus other revivalists, spent some months in the two cities; creating the breakthrough that they had been longing for. Then local evangelists came in to build on what had been done. Radcliffe organised halls to be hired in Liverpool in the autumn of 1861 and halls were also taken in Manchester. These had the same importance as they did in London, in that they enabled poor people, who never set foot in a church, to hear the gospel. The main intensity went on for about a year.

In Manchester, by October 1862, the Manchester City Mission was holding weekly 30 minute meetings amongst 40 different groups [of workers] - 4 bands of night oil men, 1 gas men, 1 lamp lighters, 1 water mains, 1 omnibus drivers, 1 carters, 9 railway porters, 4 divisions of police officers, 1 cabmen, 1 prison, 1 hospital, 2 dye works, 1 tan yard, 5 breweries, 1 steel works, 1 rope makers. As in London, they tried to reach everyone.

Around the country the Revival newspaper was often read out to encourage people, and fires were lit through the testimonies in it.

One group of evangelists were the Woolwich boys. They were from a boys' refuge and several were saved in 1859. Groups of them were invited to speak all around the country and many a fire was lit by their testimonies. Radcliffe was constantly calling for more evangelists; undoubtedly there would have been more saved in England had there been more workers.

The revival carried on in different parts of the country into 1866, The Newcastle revival was still going on in 1865.

There was a significant increase in philanthropy during this period and in years afterwards. There was a considerable down turn in the economy due to the knock on effects of the American Civil War and considerable hardship was experienced, particularly in Lancashire, so there was a considerable effort to raise money for those who were suffering.

Edwin Orr did some research to work out how many were saved in this revival in England. The figures he came up with were Church of England 250k (a calculated guess), Baptists 100k, Congregationalists 70k, Methodists 200k =

620k – Excluded from these figures would normally have been children, of whom there were many, emigrants [those who emigrated to other countries], existing members of churches who were converted in the revival and those who did not join a church." [15]

In the next chapter we will discover more about the great evangelists who were involved in bringing revival to Manchester.

3 THE MAIN EVANGELISTS

Charles Finney (1792-1875)

"Born in Warren, Connecticut, on August 29, 1792, Finney was the youngest of nine children. He was converted in 1821. Forty years later Finney recalled what happened after he had surrendered to Christ:

"The Holy Spirit descended upon me in a manner that seemed to go through me, body and soul. I could feel the impression, like a wave of electricity, going through and through me. Indeed it seemed to come in waves of liquid love, for I could not express it in any other way. It seemed like the very breath of God. I can remember distinctly that it seemed to fan me, like immense wings. No words can express the wonderful love that was spread abroad in my heart."

Immediately, he felt called to give up any idea of being a lawyer and give himself fully to the work of preaching the gospel. Indeed, he began to do just that on the very day on which he was converted, and a number of people were converted in the days that followed. When he visited his parents' home in Henderson, they were converted and others in the family also. The minister at Adams, George W Gale got him to assist in the work of the chapel, and then encouraged and helped him towards ordination, which happened in 1824. Immediately, the young Finney's preaching in the area precipitated revival.

In 1835, he became the professor of systematic theology at the newly formed Oberlin Collegiate Institute in Oberlin, Ohio." [16]

Finney was active as a revivalist from 1825 to 1835 in Jefferson County and for a few years in Manhattan. In 1830-1831, he led a revival in Rochester, New York, that has been noted as inspiring other revivals of the Second Great Awakening [in the USA]. A leading pastor in New York who was converted in the Rochester meetings gave the following account of the effects of Finney's meetings in that city: "The whole community was stirred. Religion was the topic of conversation in the house, in the shop, in the office and on the street. The only theatre in the city was converted into a livery stable; the only circus into a soap and candle factory. Grog shops [shops that sell alcohol] were closed; the Sabbath was honoured; the sanctuaries were thronged with happy worshippers; a new impulse was given to every philanthropic enterprise; the fountains of benevolence were opened, and men lived to [do] good.

In 1832 he took on the pastorate of Chatham Street Chapel in New York city, and later founded the Broadway Tabernacle. It was here towards the end of 1834 and into 1835 that he delivered a famous series of 22 weekly lectures on the subject of revival. These were subsequently published in 1835 under the title 'Lectures on Revivals of Religion'. Tens of thousands of copies of 'Lectures on Revival' were sold in America and in Britain too. In 1839 the book was translated into Welsh by Evan Griffiths, and played a significant part in the revival that spread across large parts of Wales during 1839-40. [17]

Finney, accompanied by his wife Elizabeth, paid a visit to England and Scotland in 1858-60. In December 1859 he reached Bolton (which lies about ten miles North West of Manchester, and then had a population of about 30,000). Later he went on to Manchester. Reports of these campaigns will be presented later (Chapter 4).

Reginald Radcliffe (1825-95)

"Though very few people will have heard of him today, Reginald Radcliffe was in fact probably the best known layman of his day. He worked as a solicitor and never left his secular employment until the end of his life. Nevertheless, his lifetime accomplishment was truly remarkable, considerably more than many could hope for who are in full-time ministry. As with many of his contemporaries he had little regard for denominational differences but laboured exclusively for the wider interests of the kingdom of God. He worked alongside many of the great evangelists and preachers of the day and was frequently looked to for counsel and guidance and for finding openings for the gospel, which he did very effectively. One example of this, as will be mentioned later, was when John Hambleton, whilst already engaged in fruitful ministry in Preston, had the impression laid on his heart that he should leave what he was doing and go to Manchester in the expectation of meeting Radcliffe, and to trust God to direct him through His servant. Sure enough within a few days Radcliffe arrived in Manchester from London to preach at the Corn Exchange. He informed Hambleton that God was moving in Bristol and asked both him and two of his colleagues to go there and preach to the many thousands who were expected to gather there. This happened just as he said, and a great move of God was experienced in Bristol.

Reginald Radcliffe was not a great preacher...but he was certainly an anointed one and unquestionably a God-called evangelist, seeing many thousands brought to Christ during his lifetime. This was particularly so in Aberdeen where it was said that he was the chief human agent that God used during the remarkable revival that took place there. Alvyn Austin described him as "the fiery evangelist of the 1859 revival" and Dr Howard Taylor in the book on his father, Hudson Taylor, referred to him as "that fervent evangelist whose parish was the world and whose aim was nothing less than that the Gospel should be preached to every creature." Professor Martin of Aberdeen once said of him that "he was a man who seemed to have stepped out of the days of the Acts of the Apostles amongst us. His labours were extraordinary, particularly considering that he was a layman". Reading through "The Revival" his name at times seems to appear to be mentioned on every other page, recording him preaching in some part of the country or abroad. Radcliffe was a great man of prayer and also a man of deep humility, and this was undoubtedly one of the key factors in the powerful anointing that rested on him during his lifetime. Though God used him very powerfully on a number of occasions he never allowed this in any way to affect his walk with God and remained in a position of humility and prayerfulness throughout his life.

Lady Harriet Cowper said that he had a living faith, that faith which removes mountains, which knows no obstacle, which blots out the word 'impossible' from the Christian vocabulary, because nothing is impossible with God. With great faith he would speak of his love for his Saviour and that fervent, deep and burning love for sinners, which led him to labour with such unflagging zeal for their conversion.

Enduement of power from on high [Luke 24:49] was the all-important thing to Reginald Radcliffe and also for anybody else he worked with. The following article in 'The Revival' of 21st February 1861 gives an account of a meeting of Christian workers held at the invitation of Radcliffe to pray for direction as to the means of carrying the Gospel into the thickly-peopled East of London. This is what he said to the workers:-"We do not so much want a multiplication of agents or more agencies; but there is one little word which describes our greatest need, and this is power. We want the fulfilment of the Saviour's promise, 'Ye shall receive the power of the Holy Ghost coming upon you.' Two years ago I had the privilege of asking about one hundred and twenty believers to tea. They came, not to pray for the conversion of sinners, but for power on themselves: I observed from that day one man particularly. He had been a man of God before: but thenceforward a ten-fold blessing accompanied him – souls seemed to be slain under him."

The author, R C Morgan [editor of 'The Revival' newspaper] wrote of him 'He was so filled with the Spirit that he 'bound the whole round world about the feet of God' in prayer. Prayer, prayer, prayer was the secret of his power in winning souls, and God used and honoured him to give effect to his own prayers. His frame was slight and his health weak, but he was a man of lion-like courage, of godly sincerity and with the simplicity of a child. He served his generation according to the will of God, and probably no man of his generation had done more to spread the gospel.'" [18]

Richard Weaver (1827-96)

Richard Weaver was born in Asterley, Shropshire, in 1827. He had a hard upbringing with his father being a violent man and drunkard. He became a coal miner and was himself a brutally hard man. His early days were filled with getting drunk and bare fist fighting as a semi-professional pugilist [boxer]. Through the testimonies of some Christians and especially his wife he became a Christian in 1852 and subsequently a fervent evangelist. One of the people who recognised his potential in preaching was Reginald Radcliffe who began to use him in evangelistic ministry, and acted as his mentor. At the time of the 1859 Revival he was greatly used as the rough-tongued evangelist whose preaching was readily received by the rough and ready masses of England. Vast numbers of these people were converted to Christ under his ministry. He was also a very capable soloist and used his singing talent to great effect, sometimes interrupting his own message by bursting into song.

He was powerfully used by God in the revival in Scotland during 1859. The reporter for 'The Record' [a secular newspaper] was clearly taken aback at what he saw during Radcliffe's visit to Glasgow. He wrote, 'young men and women, boys and girls, embracing each other in transports of religious delirium—swaying their bodies backwards and forwards-standing on seats and stamping their feet to the tune, and holding forth at the pitch of their voices: "Christ for Me"'(Appendix 1B).

One example of his amazing ministry was in Macclesfield in 1861 when he preached at a Methodist church, which was filled to capacity. The results were amazing with "some of the vilest characters, as well as the most intelligent people" brought to Christ. Publicans complained of their lack of customers and took down their signs. Policemen and Magistrates testified of the transformation that took place in the town's morals, with one magistrate saying that he had nothing to do on several occasions. Upwards of 1,200 converts registered with the church leaders at that place.

A report in 'The Revival' said, "Publicans are beginning to take down their signs, and others have complained that they have had no customers since Mr Weaver came. Policemen and magistrates have felt the blessed effects. One magistrate states that he has been to the bench twice during the last fortnight without having anything to do. A policeman tells us that in one street where there was perpetual brawling and fighting in the night, now you may hear nothing but the sound of prayer and praise." [19]

Richard lived in the Manchester area for much of his later life, first in Hyde and then in Hollinwood (near Oldham).

Harrison Ord (1833-1907)

Harrison Ord was born in Middlesborough on March 11, 1833. As years rolled on, young Harry developed a physique of splendid proportions, and, during his engineering apprenticeship, and subsequently, through daily contact with a lot of hard-headed men in the same workshop, he gained a strong, manly independence of character, which continued with him to the end of his earthly course, giving him, during many years of gospel work, an influence with men of a similar calibre, which many others might not wield.

Until about twenty-four years of age he lived for present things alone, although evidently bearing an excellent reputation for steady uprightness and strict morality. A successful career was his ambition...He had moved to, and was settled in, London at the time when the whole city, from its centre to its suburbs, seemed to throb with the name and fame of the young preacher, Charles Haddon Spurgeon. The month of February, 1857, had dawned, when, on a certain Sunday morning our stalwart engineer formed a unit in a crowd of 10,000 surging on toward the Surrey Gardens Music Hall.

That morning the arrow of conviction reached him, and continued to rankle in Ord's conscience, until-in a prayer-meeting not long after, when special supplication was made for him-the tale of God's love to him was told, the finished work of Christ, His willingness and power to save, the Saviour and the sinner met, the Saviour was trusted by the sinner, sorrow and sighing fled away, joy and gladness filled his heart to overflowing. The grand old hymn was at once struck up by the company, "O happy day that fixed my choice," (Appendix 1A) the voice of the young convert, as of "a son of thunder," completely drowning the combined voices of all the rest. Assured salvation, settled peace, were his from that memorable moment onward, not the shadow of a doubt ever finding a place in his mind as to "the great transaction done." (Appendix 1A verse 3)

He at once came out boldly on the Lord's side, made rapid progress in the knowledge of Christ, and of the Scriptures which testify of Him. A passionate love for the souls of his fellows possessed him, and he soon gave evidence of marked ability in preaching the gospel, much of the eloquence and force of his worthy father in the faith seeming to be inherited by the son, the voice of each being a wonder unto many.

It was not long before the bench of the engineer was forsaken for the platform of the preacher, and Harrison Ord, through his gift and grace, was speedily accorded a place in the very front ranks of the band of devoted evangelists raised up and thrust forth by the Lord of the Harvest in those early days of widespread Revival, to "gather in from the fields of sin" golden sheaves by the thousand. For some eighteen years the United Kingdom was his parish, going up and down the land in labours abundant, preaching "Christ, and Him crucified" in buildings, tents, and the open air, the Lord giving, through His servant, testimony to the word of His grace. [20]

Henry Moorhouse (1840-1880)

Henry was one of Manchester's own, and partly for this reason I will give him more attention in this book than I do to the other evangelists. Although his life was sadly short, he had a tremendous effect on the Revival both here in the UK and in the United States.

"Henry Moorhouse, or as he was more familiarly called, 'Harry Moorhouse, the English Evangelist', was born in Ardwick in the city of Manchester. When very young he was sent to jail on more than one occasion. By the age of sixteen he was a gambler, a gang leader, and was wild and beyond control. Afterwards he joined the army and tried the life of a soldier, but had to be bought out of the army by his father at considerable cost. Nonetheless, he continued with his life of drink, gambling and 'other vices'. He was suicidal and carried a gun for the purpose of killing himself should he decide to do so. [21] He once tried to poison himself.

Passing the Alhambra Circus in Manchester [in December, 1860], where Richard Weaver was preaching, hearing a noise within, and thinking a fight was going on, Henry buttoned up his coat and rushed in, ready for the fray. The place was so crowded he had to stand on the stairs. But he found he had come to a Gospel meeting. After the singing there was a Bible reading: the parable of the Prodigal Son from Luke 15, and then a sermon. Henry Moorhouse saw himself as the story was told of a rebellious, reckless youth who was far away from 'home'. The name 'JESUS' pierced his heart. His early childhood, reckless career, and awful danger rose vividly before his vision, the "Glorious gospel" (2 Cor. 4:4) message went home to his heart. Three weeks later, a friend led him to the Lord in a warehouse owned by John Rylands and Sons

[22, 23, 24].

Thus, soundly converted to God, he entered heartily into the service of his new Master. His first services were chiefly in the open air, at local and national gatherings, and in special places of concourse. From morning till evening his joy was to spend his time distributing tracts, speaking personally with individuals wherever he got an opportunity, or crying aloud in the street or market-place, urging multitudes to "flee from the wrath to come."

Like the apostle of old, he had visions of God. Upon one occasion he saw in his sleep three young men in Manchester, each strangely attired in a white jacket, on which were the words legibly written, "These men are going to Hell!" The place appeared to be near the infirmary, and before them was a deep burning lake of fire, unperceived by them. Henry called aloud for them to stop, but they took no heed, until he fell down upon his knees and cried to God, saying, "Lord, it is not by might, nor by power, but by Thy Spirit." The men then turned back in haste, having discovered their danger. This dream was on Friday night; and on the Sunday evening following, when Henry was preaching in the Alhambra Circus, those three identical young men came into the place, and before the meeting closed they were all on their knees crying out for mercy, and were brought to accept the Lord Jesus Christ and the pardon of their sins.

The revival stream, which had begun to flow in 1854, was in full tide in 1860, when Moorhouse was converted. Thus he was early brought into touch with the enthusiastic spirits-Richard Weaver, from the coalpit, whose style he largely followed; John Hambleton, the converted actor;

Edward Usher, a dockyard labourer; Wm. Carter, the converted sweep; Henry Varley, a butcher, and afterward valiant champion for the truth; Reginald Radcliffe, the Liverpool lawyer; Brownlow North, the man of wealth and fashion; Joshua Poole, better known as "Fiddler Joss; " J. Denham Smith, a devout expositor; C. H. Spurgeon, of the Metropolitan Tabernacle; H. Grattan Guinness...and many others.

The Americans D. L. Moody and Ira D. Sankey afterwards became his special friends [which will be described in Chapter 5]. Henry's special call to devote all his time to the work of the Lord came through an enthusiast known as "the hatless preacher." One evening when Henry was engaged in crying his wares as auctioneer of "Notions," [a shop in Deansgate, Manchester], the hatless man suddenly appeared before him, and cried aloud, "Thou oughtest to have thy Bible in thy hand out amongst the people, and not that hammer for the devil", and immediately departed. That short, terrible, speech was like a thunderbolt falling on Henry. He at once… went to Liverpool, sought out John Hambleton, and entered with him on an evangelistic tour through the provinces. Since that date Henry laboured in the special work of evangelizing without a fixed salary, or human promise of support. A trio consisting of Hambleton, the preacher; Edward Usher, the singer; and Henry Moorhouse, the young and fervid disciple, frequently worked together. [25]

The stories concerning the visits of these heroes to race meetings, haunts of vice, sinners in the slums; their theatre services - sometimes fourteen theatres were filled in London on one Sunday night; visits to public executions (then not uncommon); labours amongst Romanists in many parts of Ireland, and "labours more abundant" are told in "Buds, Blossoms, and Fruits of the Revival." [26] [A book written by John Hambleton.]

John Hambleton (1820-1889)

"John Hambleton...was raised in the seaport city of Liverpool, England. His saintly mother was one strong link in the events leading to his conversion. "I shall never forget the lovely way she used to place her hand upon my head, and talk about that peerless Person who was 'God manifest in the flesh'" he recounted.

But as a teenager he rebelled against his upbringing. With his peers he became an openly depraved delinquent. At sixteen he ran away from home to enter the theatre, and travel England, Australia and America as an actor, theatrical manager, adventurer, and gold digger.

The way home began in 1850 in a saloon in Geelong, Australia, when a fellow actor ridiculed the Bible. Everyone joined the laughter except John. Unable to shake off the impressions of his mother's consistent, Christ-like example and teaching, he spoke out to defend the Bible and Christianity. "In my own heart," Hambleton observed, "I believed every doctrine of the Christian faith, though I was a rejecter of Christ and a neglecter of God's great salvation."

The California gold rush drew men of Hambleton's type. Hearing about the fortunes to be had, he left Australia to go digging for something to satisfy his heart. But he would not find it in the muck of that place.

San Francisco was going through wild times. The laws allowed people to carry out, tax free, any gold they picked up, panned, or dug. Fortunes were made and lost overnight in the gold fields. Hambleton narrowly escaped alive.

He almost died several times, at least once each by drowning, stabbing, shooting, thirst, and disease. At his lowest, his 'friends' went to dig a grave while he lay nearby under a tree. "As I lay upon that grassy couch, apparently upon the eve of death, my soul trembled as conscience suggested the question, 'Where will you go when the end comes?' Then the scenes of my past life rushed with fearful imagery through my mind. I thought of the home I had deserted, of my mother's heart I had broken, the talents I had I abused, the grace of God which I had despised and rejected. And then I thought of the just retribution of the wicked and of the awful eternity, when impenitent sinners such as myself shall reap 'for ever and ever' what they have sown in time."

God had his attention, but John did not yet see the way of salvation. He recovered physically, but was still not a new creature. Circumstances came together for him to sail back home. After seventeen years absence, he stepped onto the dock at Liverpool on April 1, 1857. His quest for any relatives seemed futile. Finally, he found his sisters.

Before his mother had died years previously, she asked her daughter to write a declaration of her prayer of faith. John's sister produced the paper. One of her declarations read that God would save her prodigal son John, and bring him back to Liverpool, that he might become "a preacher of the gospel."

Determined to change, John tried the route of self-effort and for weeks he strove, struggled, vowed and resolved his way into a "Slough of Despond". Thankfully, during this time he went to a bookstore and bought a Bible. In despair of saving himself, he saw the Saviour he needed while reading John chapter 3 and 5:24.

Once he knew he was at peace with God, he wanted the same for others. "At the first my knees trembled like Jeremiah, but God directed me to His Word, saying: 'Thou shalt go to all that I shall send thee; and whatsoever I command thee thou shalt speak. Be not afraid of their faces, for I am with thee to deliver thee.'"

Reginald Radcliffe, the Liverpool lawyer, was an early encouragement to the new believer. The market place was John's brief apprenticeship in open air work. He and a dock worker named Edward Usher rented the Teutonic Hall for gospel services. It was happy work. A considerable number claimed to have been converted. Then, "with a shilling between them," he went traveling in the Name of the Lord [as an itinerant evangelist].

Reginald Radcliffe's wife says, "It was laid on the hearts of Hambleton and his friend (Usher) to go into Lancashire, and preach the gospel to some of the great populations in the towns and villages. I remember well, when they started they were going to trust God for everything. So with very little in their pockets, and hearts full of faith, they set off from Chatham Place [in Liverpool]. Mr. Radcliffe accompanied them out of town, as they went on foot. Before parting they stepped over a hedge, knelt down in the field, and commended each other and the work of God into His own keeping. Some weeks after, when they returned, they both stood up before me, and said, 'Look at us; we are better dressed than when we started, and have lacked nothing.'"

Better still, God had blessed their words to many souls. We are often told that God wants faithful servants, not necessarily successful servants. But Hambleton was both faithful and successful. The most notable success in his ministry was the men he trained. Wherever we see him, he was pushing another servant out into the work.

He urged Richard Weaver to launch out. And when the revival stream which began flowing in 1859 was at high tide, Henry Moorhouse was converted in 1861 [December 1860]. Henry came into touch with Richard (Undaunted Dick) Weaver, John Hambleton, Edward Usher, Reginald Radcliffe, and Joshua (Fiddler Joss) Poole. And there were others besides these. Sometimes these men filled fourteen rented theatres in London on one Sunday night to herald out the gospel.

When Henry Moorhouse left auctioneering to preach the gospel, the first man he went looking for was John Hambleton. Under Hambleton's wing, Henry quickly grew in grace and in the knowledge of our Lord and Saviour, Jesus Christ. Hambleton gave young Henry the "sink or swim" approach in learning how to preach the gospel. Together they entered on an evangelistic tour through the provinces. These men did their evangelizing without a fixed salary, or human promise of support. They spoke about "depending on God." It meant not depending on any denomination, organization, sect, society, or committee. John Hambleton was fearless, willing to do

God's will at all costs… He loved God's people, and they knew it." [27]

His biographer wrote "There was something in his fervid eloquence, something in the intense pathos with which he preached "The old, old story," and told about "The unsearchable riches of Christ" that arrested his hearers' attention, and left such deep and lasting impressions upon their mind." [28]

The writer Henry Pickering commented: "Amongst the gifted evangelists whom God has raised up during the last forty years are the names of three remarkable and unique men, namely, Richard Weaver, Henry Moorhouse, and John Hambleton. The trio were well known to each other, and frequently laboured together-especially in their earlier days of service-in various parts of the great harvest-field. God greatly owned and blessed their labours, and it is not too much to say that thousands of sinners were saved, and thousands of saints were helped, through their ministry." [29]

Edward Usher

I very much wanted to include a piece about Edward Usher, the close partner of John Hambleton, in this book but there is very little information available about him. We do know that Edward was born in Ireland and worked as a dockyard labourer in Liverpool before he became an evangelist. He was especially known for his hymn singing. In "Buds, Blossoms, and Fruits of the Revival" Hambleton describes how they met: "At Lime-street Lamp [in Liverpool], an old man, with white hair and feeble speech, was holding up [preaching] Jesus crucified; and when he gave out a hymn, a young Irishman, having a clear tenor voice, pitched the tune. We joined together, drew many hearers, and the hand of the Lord from that time yoked us together; for this young Irishman had been converted only a few weeks, and had been asking the Lord for a fellow-labourer who could preach in the streets; so Edward Usher's desire for a preaching man was gratified, and the writer's prayer was answered in being provided with a good singing man." After a number of fruitful years working together with Hambleton, Edward set up home with his family on Hyde Road in Manchester. He remained active as an evangelist, and had a Bible stall at Smithfield Market. He was a frequent correspondent to 'The Revival' newspaper concerning God's work in the city, as can be seen in the following chapter.

4 REVIVAL REPORTS FROM MANCHESTER AND SURROUNDING TOWNS

There isn't any continuous record of the revival in Manchester during the years 1859-62 but the following reports (mainly from 'The Revival' newspaper) provide us with some informative snapshots. These reports come from many different parts of what is now Greater Manchester, indicating that the work was very widespread.

Bolton 1860 (Charles Finney)

This account is taken mainly from Finney's own recollections [30]

"Our first meeting was in the chapel occupied by Brother Davison, who had sent for me to come to Bolton. He was an Independent, what we in this country call a Congregationalist. His chapel was filled the first night. The meeting was opened by a Methodist minister, who prayed with great fervency, and with a liberty that plainly indicated to me that the Spirit of God was upon the congregation, and that we should have a powerful meeting. I was invited to follow him with some remarks. I did so, and occupied a little space in speaking upon the subject of prayer. I tried to impress upon them as a fact that prayer would be immediately answered if they took the stumbling blocks out of the way, and offered the prayer of faith. The Word seemed to thrill through the hearts of Christians. Indeed, I have seldom addressed congregations upon any subject that seemed to produce a more powerful and salutary effect, than upon the subject of prayer. I find it so everywhere. Praying people are immediately stirred up by it to lay hold of God for a blessing. They were in this place. That was a powerful meeting.

Through the whole of that week of prayer, the Spirit of prayer seemed to be increasing, and our meetings had greater and greater power. About the third or fourth day of our meetings, I should think, it fell to the turn of a Brother Best, also a Congregational minister at Bolton, to have the meeting in his chapel. There, for the first time, I called for inquirers. After addressing the congregation for some time in a strain calculated to lead to that point, I called for inquirers, and his vestry was thronged with them. We had a powerful meeting with them, and many of them, I trust, submitted to God. There was a Temperance hall in the city, which would accommodate more people than any of the chapels. After this week of prayer the brethren secured the hall for preaching, and I began to preach there twice on the Sabbath and four evenings in the week. Soon the interest became very general. The hall would be crowded every night to its utmost capacity, so that no person could get so much as within the door. The Spirit of God was poured out copiously.

I then recommended to the brethren to canvass the whole town. To go two and two, and visit every house, and if permitted, to pray in every house in the city. They immediately and courageously rallied to perform this work.

They got great numbers of bills, and tracts, and posters, and all sorts of invitations printed, and began the work of canvassing. The Congregationalists and Methodists took hold of the work with great earnestness.

The Methodists are very strong in Bolton, and always have been since the day of Wesley. It was one of Wesley's favourite fields of labour, and they have always had there a powerful ministry and powerful churches. Their influence was far in the ascendancy there over all other religious denominations. I found among them both ministers and lay men who were most excellent and earnest labourers for Christ. But the Congregationalists too entered into the work with great spirit and energy, and while I remained there at least, all sectarianism seemed to be buried. They gave the town a thorough canvassing, and the canvassers met once or twice a week to make their reports and to consider farther arrangements for pushing the work. It was very common to see a Methodist and a Congregationalist hand in hand, and heart in heart, going from house to house with tracts, and praying wherever they were permitted in every house, and warning them to flee from the wrath to come, and urging them to come to Christ. Of course in such a state of things as this the work would spread rapidly among the unconverted. All classes of persons, high and low, rich and poor, male and female, became interested.

I was in the habit every evening I preached, of calling upon inquirers to come forward and take seats in front of the stand where I stood to preach. Great numbers would come forward, and crowd as best they could through the dense masses that stood in every nook and corner of the house. The hall was not only large on its ground floor, but had a gallery, which was always thronged to its utmost capacity. After the inquirers had come forward we always engaged in a prayer meeting, having several prayers in succession while the inquirers knelt before the Lord. The Methodist brethren were very much engaged, and were quite noisy and demonstrative in their prayers when sinners came forward. For some time I said nothing about this, lest I should throw them off and lead them to grieve the Spirit. I saw that their impression was, that the greater the excitement the more rapidly would the work go forward. They therefore would pound the benches, pray exceedingly loud, and sometimes more than one at a time. I was aware that this distracted the inquirers, and prevented their becoming truly converted; and although the number of inquirers was great and constantly increasing, yet conversions did not multiply as fast as I had been in the habit of seeing them, even where the number of inquirers was much less.

After letting things pass on so for two or three weeks until the Methodist brethren had become acquainted with me, and I with them, after calling the inquirers forward one evening I suggested that we should take a different course. I told them that I thought the inquirers needed more opportunity to think than they had when there was so much noise. That they needed instruction, and needed to be led by one voice in prayer at a time; and that there should not be any confusion, or anything bordering on it, if we expected them to listen and become intelligently converted. I asked them if they would not try for a short time to follow my advice in that respect, and see what the result would be. They did so; and at first I could see that they were a little in bondage when they attempted to pray, and a little discouraged because it so crossed their ideas of what constituted powerful meetings. However, they soon seemed to recover from this, because I think they were convinced that although there was less apparent excitement in our prayer meetings, yet there were many more converted from evening to evening."

In Bolton, Elizabeth Finney also found greater scope for ministry among the women. Her journals of the period show both she and her husband too have been extremely busy, and the meetings long and protracted. The Finney team was clearly working very effectively, and in the three and a half months they were in Bolton they saw much success: there were over two thousand enquirers and 1,200 converts - which amounts to a significant proportion of the total population.

"The fame of this work spread abroad, and soon they began to come in large numbers from Manchester to Bolton to attend our meetings; and this, as was always the case, created a considerable excitement in that city, and a desire to have me come there as soon as I could.

However, I remained in Bolton I think about three months, perhaps more. The work became so powerful that it broke in upon all classes, and every description of persons. It extended to the factories, or cotton mills, as they were called. Brother Barlow had an extensive mill in Bolton, and employed a great many hands, male and female. I called with him down to his mill once or twice, and held meetings with his operatives. The first time we went we had a powerful meeting. I remained with them till I was much fatigued, and then returned home, leaving Brother Barlow still to pray with and instruct them. When he came home he reported that not less than sixty appeared clearly to be converted that evening among his own hands [workers]. Thus meetings were continued till nearly all his hands expressed hope in Christ.

There were a great many very striking cases of conviction and conversion at the time. Although I kept cool myself, and endeavoured to keep the people in an attitude in which they would listen to instruction, and would act understandingly in everything they did; still in some instances persons for a few days were too much excited for the healthy action of their minds, though I do not recollect any case of real insanity. One night as I was standing on the platform and preaching, a man in the congregation rose up and crowded his way up on the platform and said to the congregation, "I have committed a robbery." He began to make a confession, interrupting me as I was preaching. I saw that he was overexcited, and Brother Davison who sat on the platform stepped up and whispered to him, and took him down into a side room and conversed with him. He found that he had committed a crime for which he was liable to be transported [to Australia]. He gave him advice, and I heard no more of it that evening. Afterwards the facts came out more fully to my knowledge. But in a few days the man obtained a hope.

The work went on there and spread until one of the ministers who had been engaged in engineering the movement of canvassing the town, said publicly in my presence, that they found that the revival had reached every family in the city; and that every family had been visited, I think he said more than once. Indeed they kept up the visitation whilst I remained there, and thoroughly canvassed the town.

If we had had any place of worship that could have held the inhabitants of the town, we should probably have had ten thousand persons there from evening to evening. All we could do was to fill the hall as full as it could crowd, and then use such other means as we could to reach the multitudes in other places of worship."

Manchester 1860 (Charles Finney)

"In April we went to Manchester... As is well-known, the manufacturing districts have a stronger democratic element than other parts of England. Congregationalism, therefore, is more popular in Manchester than in any other city that I visited. I had not been long there, however, before I saw that there was a great lack of mutual confidence among the brethren there. I could see that there was [disunity] among the leaders in that movement, and frequently to my grief I heard expressions that indicated a lack of real heart-union in the work. This, I was soon convinced, was a great difficulty to be overcome, and that if it could not be overcome, the work could never be as general there as it had been in Bolton. There soon was manifest a dissatisfaction with some of the men who had been selected to engineer the work -to get out the bills, do the necessary printing, and provide for carrying on the general movement. This grieved the Spirit and crippled the work. And although from the very first the Spirit of God attended the Word, yet the work never so thoroughly overcame the sectarian feeling and disagreements of the brethren generally, that it could spread over the city in the way it had done at Bolton. When I went to that city I expected that the Methodist and Congregational brethren would work harmoniously together, as they had at Bolton, but in this I found myself mistaken. Not only was there a want of cordiality and sympathy between the Methodists and Congregationalists, but also a great lack of confidence and sympathy amongst the Congregationalists themselves. However, our meetings were very interesting, and great numbers of inquirers were found on every side; and whenever a meeting was appointed for inquirers, large numbers would attend. Still, what I longed to see was a general overflowing of the Spirit's influences in Manchester, as we had witnessed it in Bolton.

After labouring in Manchester proper for several weeks, we made a stand at Salford - which is, indeed, a part of Manchester. I spent most of my time after that in Salford and Pendleton.

We continued in Manchester till about the first of August, and the revival continued to increase and spread up to that time." [31]

After spending 18 months in England and Scotland getting the revival going, the Finneys returned to the United States. Although the Finneys' work in Manchester was not the unqualified success it was in Bolton (because of disunity), it nevertheless laid the foundation for local evangelists to build on. Some of these (like Radcliffe and Weaver) had been powerfully used in the revival in Scotland in 1859, but returned to work in England, first in London and then in Lancashire, in the following years. The revival fire really took hold during 1861 and 1862.

Manchester Corn Exchange 1861

On Sunday, the 15th of September our dear friend Mr Radcliffe again delivered the addresses afternoon and evening in the Corn Exchange, which was filled on both occasions. Though he was so unwell as to be hardly fit to be out of bed, he spoke with great affection and earnestness on the love of God to sinners. And it was manifest that the divine word was with almighty power, for a number of persons remained to be conversed with after both services. At the close of the afternoon address, one young woman in the anteroom burst forth in praise to God for his pardoning grace to her own soul and then most fervently wrestled in prayer for the salvation of her sister and another relative. It was a deeply moving scene.

From, "The Revival", volume V, 5th October 1861.

He [Radcliffe] experienced much blessing in Manchester whilst speaking in various chapels, which were crowded to capacity. In one of these meetings a group of volunteers left during the service and went down into the back streets where there were none but thieves and prostitutes and numbers of them came back to the chapel and were converted. Also on this occasion a backslider, who heard this group singing in the streets where the brothels were, was convicted of his sin and began to weep. He followed the group back to the chapel and re-dedicated his life to the Lord again. Such was the blessing experienced in Manchester at that time that a special meeting was held in the Corn Exchange for all the converts and those still anxious about their souls and it was crowded to excess with around 2000 people being present.

Our dear brother Richard Weaver writes:

"My dear Brother in Christ,--You will be rejoiced to hear that I have got a most blessed movement in this city. All glory to God, for He does all things well! I have been in the Corn Exchange all this week with great crowds, and many poor sinners every night seeking Jesus their Saviour. The city seems to be on the move, and the children crying, "Give me [spiritual] bread to eat", and, bless God, Jesus is the bread of life, and many poor sinners are beginning to eat and live. My health has been very bad this week. I have not been able to stop till the close of the meeting, but from all sides there is good news coming to me of drunkards, and harlots of the streets, and infidels, and sinners of all characters finding pardon through the blood of the Lamb. A brother told me today that he knows a great many young men that have been infidels have been converted, and he is going to get them to write some letters to me. Glory to God, sin must be swept away when the blood of the Lamb is sprinkled on the hearts of sinners. "Christ must reign," says the Bible, and I believe it. I feel quite glad that God has brought me to this city. If you could but see the people coming out to hear God's word here you would be delighted. Men from their workshops with their dirty faces now can say; the blood of Jesus has cleansed their sins away. All glory to the bleeding Lamb! A friend said to me about two years ago, "Manchester people are a hard lot of people," and he thought he should never preach there again. But, thank God, the Holy Ghost has found a way to the hearts of some of the hardest. I shall not write much at this time, but send you a few copies of letters that I have received while here. I feel, dear brother, nearly done, I am so weak. Do pray for me. The Lord is my strength and my salvation. You must pray for me; I need your prayers. Victory through the blood of the Lamb. Yours ever in Christ, RICHARD WEAVER."

From 'Revival Newspaper', volume V, page 134. Oct 26th, 1861.

REVIVAL IN MANCHESTER

"The work begun last September in this great city is rolling on, and since I last wrote to you, several fresh halls, rooms, and cottage-meetings have been opened, and every seat occupied, and not a week passes but souls are born of God. The meetings in the Corn Exchange are very much blessed of the Lord, and there is not a Sabbath passes but there are many anxious souls, and many professed to find peace and joy in believing. On Monday there is a meeting for converts; I am happy to say that about 100 assemble to be fed with the milk of the word, and it is a time of refreshing to be assembled with these lambs of the flock. The room that was taken in Hyde-street, Ardwick, mentioned in *The Revival,* becoming too small, the brother that paid for it said if one could be got that would hold a thousand he would bear all expense. After some time one was procured, and I am glad to say that it is too small and could not hold the people on last Sabbath night. It is most remarkable to see this congregation of young converts, some of whom were the most abandoned characters. Infidels, boxers, drunkards, thieves, clothed and in their right mind, sitting at the feet of Jesus, Well may the saints of God sing:

"Jesus is worthy to *receive*
Honour and power divine;
And blessings more than we can give
Be, Lord, forever thine."

In this same room there is a prayer-meeting of boys, and from 100 to 150 assembled, and it is most encouraging to hear these little ones pour out their hearts for the conversion of their drunken fathers, and unconverted mothers and sisters and brothers, and for a Revival of God's work. There is also a prayer-meeting held on

Sabbath morning at seven o'clock, and from fifty to seventy meet to pour out their hearts to the Lord for a blessing on this city and the country. There are several other meetings held, such as a Bible-class, and meetings for exhortation during the week, and also cottage-meetings in various parts of the neighbourhood, as a young convert calls them, kindling little fires in every street.

From 'The Revival', Volume VI, page 102. [32]

Free Trade Hall 1861

The meetings in the Free Trade Hall with Reginald Radcliffe were a complete success; it was crowded to [excess]. Many were broken down [with conviction of sin].

The visit of Richard Weaver is very opportune, succeeding Mr Radcliffe's recent meetings in Manchester; and great hopes are entertained by many of a widely extended blessing. We were much struck, at both meetings in the Free Trade Hall, with a large proportion of men. Weaver noticed it at the evening meeting, saying it was a good sign for Manchester, for if the men came the women would follow.

From, 'The Revival', Volume V, 19th October 1861

(By Richard Weaver) I now write to you to let you know that God is still with me and blessing his word to the salvation of precious souls. All glory to his name. I have had some good meetings at Manchester and many sinners found peace with God there. One man took hold of my hand and said with tears in his eyes, "the Lord bless you, Mr Weaver, did you ever came to Manchester; for before you came to the city I was an infidel but I came to hear you; the Lord convinced me of my error and bless God now I can say, 'Christ for me' (Appendix 1B), for the Lord has pardoned all my sins and my home is like a little heaven, for my wife has found the Lord as well; bless His name. Oh Mr Weaver the Lord bless you, for I know that I am a sinner saved and washed by the blood of the Lamb." Last Sunday night, a Roman Catholic got up on the form after I had done speaking and said, "thank God that I ever came to hear Mr Weaver, with some more of my friends who are Roman Catholics, for we have found that it is not beads, nor Saints nor crucifixes, nor anything else, but it's Christ and him alone, that can save; and thank God I with some of my fellow workmen can say that the Lord has forgiven us and given us peace in Christ; and we were pleased with the discourses and especially with God, who so loved the world and I know many Roman Catholics and bigoted ones, that are thankful to God that they came to the Free Trade Hall." So you see, the Lord is doing wonders in this great city; all glory to the Lamb; for the gospel is getting the victory over hell and devils, and it's saving sinners.

From, 'The Revival', Volume V, 30th November 1861. [33]

Rochdale 1860-61

1860. The chapel was built [in 1837] by those who had withdrawn their membership from the Wesleyan Methodist Association. They wanted to do some evangelising of the area, and so invited [James] Caughey. The meetings were advertised in the Rochdale Observer, and 2,000 handbills were printed. At the first service, 24 were justified and 21 sanctified [34]. The leaders kept extending the dates until Whitsun (late April), by when 1,800 had been justified and sanctified. The leadership were very grateful to Caughey and tried, unsuccessfully, to persuade him to return when Caughey came back to England in 1867. From the chapel register it appears that there were few backsliders.

Taken from 'Holding the Fort' by John Kent, pages 82-87 [35]

1861. Dr and Mrs Palmer [American evangelists] have been here. 570 names have been enrolled for visitation and pastoral care, the fruit of their visit; they have now left us, and Richard Weaver has been preaching to 2000 every night. Old and young, notorious sinners and backsliders, are yielding to the truth. The Church is stirred up. To come up to the help of the Lord against the mighty is felt to be a solemn responsibility. "Each one must build against his own house and each one must do his own work", and wait daily upon God to know what that work is, and, with willing hearts, seek for the grace to do it.

From the 'Revival Newspaper', Volume IV, p 103. [36]

Salford 1861

On Wednesday, 18th September, 1861, the Presbyterian Free Church in Salford was occupied. As on the preceding night, there was a good many anxious souls; at the close, nearly the whole congregation remained for conversation. The scene was now most solemn. In every part of the church were to be seen anxious persons weeping over their sins and asking what they must do to be saved. A soldier stood up and modestly declared what great things God had done for his soul; how at one of these meetings he was brought to see the error of his way and to flee to Jesus; and now he was rejoicing in a covenant Saviour. Another soldier also rose up and urged his mates to turn at once to the Lord. Many were melted to tears by the simple story of redeeming love as told by these men and by others in the meeting. The vestry and school room also filled with anxious enquirers and not a few seemed that night to pass from death unto to life. Mr Reginald Radcliffe has been greatly encouraged by the signs of awakening in Manchester.

From, 'The Revival', Volume V, 5th October 1861. [37]

Hyde c. 1860

(By John Hambleton) It now pleased the Lord to lead John Latham, one of the Liverpool band, to give up his trade of cigar-making, and go forth without purse or scrip to preach the gospel. He followed us to Manchester, where he laboured success fully in cottage-meetings and sick visitations, the Lord supplying his daily need, as He had done ours. Mr. H., being a member of the British and Foreign Bible Society, he was used as a key to open that door for Edward and myself, as the Lord had work for us to carry Bibles and Testaments into the market-places of Lancashire; thus, while preaching the gospel, by circulating the Scriptures, we could provide things honest by our own labour. Its beginning was small, but its latter end has been greatly increased. In a railway-train, one morning, as we offered the Testament for fourpence, a gentleman in the carriage, from Hyde, asked us some questions, and hearing we were from Liverpool, where the revival had been going on, invited us to his town, as there were to be 'wakes' [local holidays] held there on the next day. This was the Lord's leading, for there was a rough collier down in the bowels of the earth whom no one knew anything about; but as the Lord must needs go through Samaria to convert a poor woman, so He must send us through Hyde, in

Cheshire, to bring Richard Weaver out of the pit; for the great revival was not to end at Liverpool or Manchester, nor were the few labourers now raised up the only company to be engaged in this mighty ingathering of souls which had only just begun.

John Street fell in with the work in good earnest. He had a little stall made, and Hyde market-place was the first stand we took with the stall. The Lord began to work mightily in this place; souls were converted at their fire sides and in the open air. On Saturday evening, some colliers who had been converted, and belonged to the Primitive Methodist Connexion, came to help us to sing, and we were glad of their help. They had loud voices, and sang genuine songs of Zion. One of them began to speak a little, which told us he had a gift for outdoor work. On the following Good Friday an announcement was made that some of the ministers would come and help us in an open-air meeting. John Latham came up from Manchester, but not a single minister was to be seen. An immense crowd had gathered from the country round, and when we were finishing, Edward [Usher] saw the collier, who had before spoken, in the crowd. He beckoned him up, and told the people one of their fellow-workmen would now address them. This was the first public assembly Richard Weaver had addressed. [38]

Oldham and Wigan c. 1860

(By Edward Usher and John Hambleton) At Oldham, while singing in the street to attract the crowd, that the gospel might be preached, hundreds of factory children, having learned the hymns, walked hand in hand, and sang with them at the lamp-post, where they remained until after the preaching; they sang again on their way down to a school kept by a Christian lady, who though in poor circumstances herself took them in and gave them lodging. Meetings were being held in her school and God gave such power to the Word that the children from the factories were converted and parents were subsequently converted through their children. Thus a great work went on and many people were brought to know the Lord.

In Wigan, it was a blessed sight to see the tears coursing down the black faces of those rough colliers, as they stood around the lamp in the open market; and no place does the writer remember where such simplicity of character lay buried beneath a rough exterior, as at this town. Hundreds received the Word during the twelve months we laboured here, and thousands of copies of the Scriptures were circulated. At this town we tried the experiment of forming a meeting for the breaking of bread, according to the simple order left on record of the early Church—teaching them to continue "in the apostles' doctrine and fellowship, and in breaking of bread, and in prayers" (Acts ii. 42). These four things in simplicity, without building temples, we saw to be the Scriptural Church order in this dispensation. While we stayed at Wigan, it was most blessed, with the presence of the Lord Jesus as our only Lord and Master; but there were no gifted pastors already taught in the Word, and our call was that of fishermen more than shepherds. We had to remove to other waters. We put the Bible into their hands, told them to search for themselves, and take heed to their lives by faith and prayer, and left them in the hands of the Lord, who had begun a good work, and would continue it.

They cried like little children the morning we took our

leave of them. There were husbands and wives who now had happy homes, where previously poverty, drunkenness, misery, and sin had reigned. [39]

Ancoats 1861

Dear Sir,—The Sabbath meetings in Manchester continue crowded to excess, and fruits are gathered which make the heart rejoice. Last Sabbath… Mr [Reginald] Radcliffe, whose will to work is greater far than his bodily strength, addressed two vast assemblages with great power and effect. The Lord was manifestly present, and after the evening service the two large ante-rooms were filled with those anxious to be conversed with and pointed to Christ. Some had their convictions deepened, some their doubts removed, and many went away feeling it was good to be there. On the following Wednesday evening, a meeting was held in Chalmers' Presbyterian Church, Ancoats. It was well attended, but it was more remarkable for its character than its numbers. I have seen a good deal of this work, but I must say it has not fallen to my lot to witness such a meeting, to see so many who, when the question was put to them, could say that they had found Christ, and were happy in Him. Nor was it the confession of the mouth only; very many faces beamed with unmistakable delight, and betokened a peace in the Soul which the world can neither give nor take away. The mere on-looker could say, "Behold how they love one another". Many came long distances to be present at this prayer-meeting though neither Mr Weaver nor Mr Radcliffe was to be there. They came to meet with God's people, and what was better, to meet with Christ.

From, 'Revival Newspaper' Volume V, page 164, Nov 23rd, 1861. [40]

Harpurhey 1861

During the past ten weeks a very refreshing and successful series of Revival services have been held daily, in connexion chiefly with Union Chapel (Independent and Baptist) and the Primitive Methodists. Meetings for supplication have been held in the dinner-hour daily in the Independent-school-room or in the Primitive Methodist chapel; these have been well attended and very encouraging, and services every night. Considerable numbers from surrounding places have received spiritual benefit, and many of all ages and both sexes profess to have come into the glorious liberty of the children of God. The influence on the young has been very delightful, and the Sabbath-schools have been both increased and improved. Salvation has come to many a house hitherto without God, and a holy stimulus has been imparted to many a fainting Christian soul. Two features about the services have been very interesting. First, the movement has been eminently unsectarian. Opportunity has been given to Christian men of good character, and acceptable gifts from various Christian denominations, to take an active part in it, which they have profitably done. Hence, secondly, the good work has been a company, a co-operative one; no one person has been the main instrument. Christian reader, pray that the young converts may be strengthened in the faith and that our city of Manchester and our important county of Lancashire may speedily enjoy "showers of blessings". E. H. WEEKS.

From the 'Revival Newspaper', Volume IV, p. 119. [41]

Duckinfield 1861

From this place we hear of special services carried on week after week and attended with much blessing. Our correspondent says: "There is a glorious work going on; sinners are smitten on every hand. Infidels boldly oppose, laughing to scorn those who in earnest seek salvation; but, thanks be to God, He giveth us the victory through our Lord Jesus Christ; in spite of all opposition, seeking souls come forward and cast themselves on the Lord."

From the 'Revival Newspaper', Volume V, p. 198. [42]

Cockerhill (Stalybridge) 1861

During the last three weeks the Lord has graciously owned the labours of Thomas Wood, a converted bricklayer on Cockerhill. Prayer-meetings are held from house to house during the week, and much good has been done. Some have bid farewell to the public-houses, the card-table, gambling, cock-fighting, dancing, pigeon-flying, etc., etc., and are not ashamed to stand up and tell what the Lord has done for their souls. During the past week fifty-three have been converted to God. Children are praying for God to touch the hearts of their drunken fathers and mothers and singing:

"Happy day, happy day!
When Jesus washed my sins away." (Appendix 1A)

Your prayers are requested for a man who threw a gallon of ale on us at a meeting last Tuesday night. He could not stand to hear his children praying for him in the street. We hope to see him pull down his sign-board shortly. May the power of God touch his heart. Brethren, pray for the quickening of the churches in this wicked town and for a greater awakening among the ungodly. Thank God I ever went to the Corn Exchange,

Manchester, to hear Richard Weaver. He stirred me up to seek the conversion of my sinful neighbours. All glory to God, He is moving powerfully among them.

From the 'Revival Newspaper', Volume V, p. 165.

The work of the Lord is still prospering on Cockerhill. During the past week one hundred and ten persons have given their names as professedly pardoned sinners. A young man came to mock, but the Lord touched his heart, and he found pardon and peace; he brought his father, mother, sister, and brother, and they all professed to obtain the blessing they sought — their house has become a house of prayer. God is working powerfully among the vilest sinners in the town; drunkards, gamblers, Sabbath-breakers, etc., attend our meetings, and a great many have turned to God and are singing nightly that beautiful hymn, "Christ for me." (Appendix 1B).

One old man says his heart is burning with the love of Jesus the same as if he had the heart-burn; another man who had been a great drunkard, now kneels down with his wife to pray and praise the Lord for what He has done for him and his family. Another young convert, a noted card-player, addressed his ungodly companions on Monday night last; after the meeting twenty-six gave their names as having been turned from darkness to light. They went home at ten o'clock, singing, "My old companions, fare you well." Pray for us.

From the 'Revival Newspaper', Volume V, p. 199. [43]

Smithfield Market (1862)

(By Edward Usher) It is most [encouraging] to me, as I stand at the Bible stall in Smithfield market to hear the testimony of thieves, infidels, gamblers, drunkards and others who have been brought to the knowledge of the Lord during the last three months of the past year and though dear Weaver and Radcliffe and Ord are gone, yet the work of Grace is extending through the city and rooms are being opened every week for prayer and praise. You are aware that we have not any mighty or noble amongst us in this work, but it seems that the Lord is using the foolish things of this world to confound the mighty and this is one feature in the present revival, that it is of God. Many of the Lord's people here look on with great suspicion and are neutral in this glorious work, because it did not come through the ordained ministry; but if any dear brother doubts the work here or the statements that have been made in the revival paper ['The Revival'], I stand daily in Smithfield market and can give hundreds of witnesses of souls being saved through the blood of the Lamb, or in reply to letters addressed to 113, Hyde Road, Manchester. I wish to give you a little information in respect of the circulation of the Scriptures, in connection with the revival movement. When first I met Richard Weaver, it was in Hyde market, near Manchester at the Bible stall and from that period up to the present the revival has spread through England, Ireland and Scotland and many of the Lord's people who have read [the book about] Weaver's life and the revival paper ['The Revival'], will see that this statement is correct. Since that time I have visited and stood with the bible stall in markets, wakes, fairs, races etc., exhibiting suitable passages of scripture to catch the eye of the multitudes of people as they are bent on pleasure. Hundreds of thousands of tracks have been distributed. We have sold upwards of 29,760 copies of the Scriptures during this period and who will deny that this is a work of God, and the good that may result from the circulation of the word of life among a class of people who never go to church or chapel, will only be known by Him who giveth the increase. Public houses, beer shops and brothels have been visited and a very important work has been undertaken in the visitation of factories and foundries during dinner hour. Thousands of copies of the Scriptures have been purchased and great good has resulted from this agency.

From, 'The Revival', Volume VI, 25th Jan 1862. [44]

Alhambra Circus (Portland Street) 1862

(By Edward Usher) This is a very good account of what went into the summer meetings during the revival.

Prior to this, by posters and advertisements, the public had been informed that Lieutenant Rochfort and Joseph Woodhouse of Cavendish technical college, would address meetings in the Corn Exchange and the Alhambra Circus, and a good brother having printed 10,000 small bills, with a similar announcement, the people of the Lord went in various parts of the highways and hedges to command the people to Lieutenant Rochfort to come and hear the word of life. In Campfield fairground, Mr Usher and others gathered a great company, urged them to flee from sin, told them of the happiness of that man whose sin was forgiven and pointed them to an all-sufficient Saviour. Here the Lord was with them, and testimony was given at night by Mr Usher of one who said, "I have often driven men to the racecourse in my cart for the devil, but I feel that I have been snatched from the brink of ruin and will now serve Jesus Christ." This man is now clothed and in his right mind, sitting at the feet of Jesus. Open-air meetings were again held, previous to the Corn Exchange afternoon service, with a view to fill that place of worship and accordingly, at a given time, the Lord's people sang through the streets and lanes leading to the Exchange, bringing with them a large number of people anxious to hear the gospel of Jesus Christ.

The Exchange service was commenced by Mr Crane, who regretted that in consequence of overpowering exertions in Yorkshire, where he has laboured with a blessed influence, he was unable to take so active a part as he wished in the services. Lieutenant Rochfort, however, contrary to his doctor's orders, was present and briefly though faithfully and touchingly addressed the assembly. Mr Joseph Woodhouse next addressed the meeting. He showed the universal Dominion of sin, its origin in thought and its development into practice. Sin, he showed, existed in proportion to man's ignorance of God, that it was realised by man's natural desires, increased by fellowship with sinners and perpetuated by the stratagems of the devil. The wrath of...God and the awful doom of the impenitent was described with much power, and the love and compassion of Jesus tenderly urged. Shortly after the afternoon service, meetings were again held in the open air. A goodly company listened attentively to the word of grace and many of them joined in singing through Drone Gate, Peter Street and thence to the Alhambra Circus, a comfortable building in Portland Street, sitting upwards of 2000 people. Dr Leadward, previous to opening the service by singing and prayer, announced that the Circus had been opened to afford greater accommodation for the special religious service which originated from the daily prayer meetings. This was the first service held in the Circus; but, judging from the exceedingly large attendance, the Circus will be kept open for some weeks, in addition to the Exchange, Fairfield Street and other rooms and he believed it would be consecrated to God by the awakening of many souls from death to life. Mr Joseph Woodhouse was then called upon to address the assembly. A gracious influence pervaded the meeting and the weeping and frequent responses of the congregation testified that the Lord was working powerfully among the people. No meetings since the visit of Richard Weaver has been so abundantly blessed by God in Manchester, as the service in the Circus last Sabbath evening. Numbers of weeping supplicants prostrated themselves before God and pleaded for pardon. Many found consolation in Jesus Christ, and at the close of the service hundreds of people assembled in front of the circle singing, with joyful hearts, praising the Almighty God. At the close of the service many remained for prayer.

From, 'The Revival', Volume VI, 19th June 1862 [45]

The revival in Manchester did not ebb away quickly, and the work continued on in the following years…

Manchester 1863

(By Edward Usher) "I am…glad to inform you that Mr. Elwin and Robert Craig [evangelists] have been labouring in Manchester and the various towns, and they have been received by the people gladly. In almost all the towns in Lancashire the Lord has opened a door for the preaching of the word. The harvest is very great, but we need labourers and means [finance], so that neutral ground may be provided for the hundreds that throng to hear the gospel of the grace of God."

From 'The Revival', Volume VI, 12th February 1863.

Summary

"In the 1859 Revival God visited the whole of the UK with a wonderful revival, which affected virtually the whole of the country. In Ulster this was indeed very dramatic with a large percentage of the population brought to Christ within that year. This was followed in a similar way in Wales and Scotland, but in most of England it was slower and less dramatic, but the end result was just the same, with some 600,000 brought to Christ in England during the period 1859-1864. In London and most of England (including Liverpool and Manchester) it was mainly a revival of preaching, preceded by a large-scale prayer movement that lasted some two years, with God raising up a vast army of evangelists, who preached the gospel throughout the land so powerfully." [46].

And yet, there was more to come...

5 D. L. MOODY AND HENRY MOORHOUSE

"Dwight Lyman Moody was born in 1837 at Northfield, Massachusetts, into a Unitarian bricklayer's family. His father died when Moody was 4, leaving nine children for his mother, Betsey, to raise. His mother never encouraged Dwight to read the Bible, and he only acquired the equivalent of a fifth-grade education [comparable to UK year 6]. He struck out on his own at age 17 and sold shoes in his uncle's Boston store. He also attended YMCA and Sunday school classes, where he became a Christian at age 18. Shortly after that, he moved to Chicago, where he sold shoes and worked toward his goal of amassing a fortune of $100,000.

It slowly dawned on Moody that, in light of his new faith, his life should not be spent on amassing wealth as much as on helping the poor. In 1858 he established a mission Sunday school at North Market Hall in a slum of Chicago. It soon blossomed into a church (from which, six years later, was formed the Illinois Street Independent Church, precursor to the now famous Moody Memorial Church). By 1861 he had left his business to concentrate on social and evangelistic work.

As president of the Chicago YMCA for four years, he

championed evangelistic causes such as distributing tracts all over the city, and he held daily noon prayer meetings. During the Civil War, he refused to fight, saying, "In this respect I am a Quaker," but he worked through the YMCA and the United States Christian Commission to evangelize the Union troops. He relentlessly sought and received financial support for all his projects from rich Christian businessmen, such as Cyrus McCormick and John Wanamaker. In all this, he tried to mix effective social work with evangelism.

The Great Chicago Fire in October 1871 destroyed Moody's mission church, his home, and the YMCA. He travelled to New York to raise funds to rebuild the church and the YMCA, but while walking down Wall Street, he felt what he described as "a presence and power" such as he had never known before, so much so that he cried aloud, "Hold Lord, it is enough!" Following this fresh anointing with the Holy Spirit, he returned to Chicago with a new vision: preaching the Kingdom of God, not social work, would change the world. He now devoted his immense energies solely to the 'evangelization of the world in this generation'" [47].

***

Through incessant labours in Britain, the Manchester evangelist Henry Moorhouse, began to show signs of badly needing rest and change. Hence he set out for the United States, arriving in Philadelphia in 1868. His welcome was so hearty, and his ministry so appreciated, that he paid five visits in the following ten years. How he became "the man who moved the man who moved the world" [or sometimes "the man who moved the man who moved millions"] is best told in D. L. Moody's own words: "In

1867, when I was preaching in Dublin, at the close of the service a young man, who did not look over seventeen [he looked very youthful and was sometimes known as "the boy preacher"], though he was older, came up to me and said he would like to go back to America with me, and preach the gospel. I thought he could not preach it, and I said I was undecided when I could go back. He asked me if I would write to him, as I did not know whether I wanted him or not. After I arrived at Chicago I got a letter saying he had just arrived in New York, and he would come and preach. I wrote him a cold letter, asking him to call on me if he came West. A few days after I got a letter stating he would be in Chicago next Thursday. I didn't know what to do with him. I said to the officers of the Church, 'There is a man coming from England, and he wants to preach. I am going to be absent Thursday and Friday. If you will let him preach on those days I will be back on Saturday and take him off your hands.' They did not care about his preaching, being a stranger; but at my request they let him preach."

When Moody returned he asked his wife, "Well, what about that young preacher?"

"Oh, he is a better preacher than you are."

"Why?" said Moody.

"He is telling sinners that God loves them".

"He is wrong! God doesn't love sinners!"

"Well, go and hear him." replied his wife.

"Why? Is he still preaching?" asked Mr. Moody.

"Yes, he has been preaching all week and has taken only one text, John 3:16."

As Moody listened he discovered Moorhouse was still on the same text, and that souls were being wonderfully saved. Moody confided to a friend, "I never knew up to that time that God loved us so much. This heart of mine began to thaw out; I could not keep back the tears. I just drank it in. So did the crowded congregation. I tell you there is one thing that draws above everything else in the world and that is love."

Mr. Moody was present at the meeting when Moorhouse got up and said, "I have been hunting and hunting all through the Bible looking for a text, and I think we will just talk about John 3:16 once more." Mr. Moody always testified that it was on that night that he got his first clear understanding of the gospel and the love of God.

On one occasion, young Moorhouse challenged Moody, "You are sailing on the wrong tack. If you will change your course, and learn to preach God's words instead of your own, He will make you a great power [for good]."

Moody's evangelistic preaching was to take on a different tenor than that of so much previous revivalistic preaching in the American tradition. From that point on there was… a new emphasis on God's love for the sinner. "*This is a faithful saying, and worthy of all acceptance: Christ Jesus came into the world to save sinners* (1 Timothy 1:15)" [48].

Moody was deeply moved by Moorhouse's preaching. "In closing up that seventh sermon, he said, 'for seven nights I have been trying to tell you how much God loves you, but this poor stammering tongue of mine will not let me. If I could ascend Jacob's ladder and ask Gabriel, who stands in the presence of the Almighty, to tell me how much love God the Father has for this poor lost world, all that Gabriel could say would be, that 'God so loved the world, that He gave His only begotten Son, that whosoever believeth in Him should not perish, but have everlasting life'. I have never forgotten those nights. I have preached a different gospel since, and I have had more power with God and man since then." [49]

Henry also encouraged the evangelistic work of the singer Ira Sankey, whom he met in Chicago in 1872. Sankey said: "It was he who first suggested the thought of going across the sea [the Atlantic] to sing the Gospel" [50]. Ever after he was a close, personal friend and helper of Messrs. Moody and Sankey, assisting them in many evangelistic campaigns.

Moody has been fairly described as "The greatest evangelist of the 19th Century" [51]. He paid several visits to Great Britain, with many millions hearing the gospel from his lips in this country alone.

Almost certainly, it was with the encouragement of Henry Moorhouse that Moody and Sankey visited Manchester during their great gospel campaign in Britain and Ireland in the years 1873-75.

6 1874: THE REVIVAL WITH MOODY AND SANKEY

The period 1859-74 was not one of a continuous revival in Manchester, but one of two waves of revival. The first, in 1859-62, had not fully ebbed away before the second wave came rushing in with the visit of D. L. Moody and Ira Sankey in 1874. Moody spoke these words on the eve of his campaign in Newcastle-on-Tyne in 1873: "We are on the eve of a great revival which may cover Great Britain, and perhaps make itself felt in America. And why may not the fire burn as long as I live? When this revival spirit dies, may I die with it." [52]

After spending time bringing revival to the North East of England (where Henry Moorhouse assisted them), and then in Scotland and Ireland, Moody and Sankey arrived in Manchester at the end of November 1874. There they spent a whole month holding daily services in the Free Trade Hall. Thankfully, there was a lot more unity among the churches at this time, compared to Finney's visit fourteen years earlier. Here are some highlights from the Manchester campaign, as recorded in the book "Narrative of Messrs. Moody and Sankey's Labors in Scotland and Ireland. Also, in Manchester, Sheffield and Birmingham,

England." [53] (Appendix 1C-E contains examples of hymns sung at this time.)

"Our dear brethren [Moody and Sankey] have come among us in dark, wintry weather, but there has been no gloom or coldness in any of their meetings, nor have rain or fog diminished the crowds that flocked to hear them. They have evidently come "in the fullness of the blessing of the gospel of Christ" and they have found awaiting them, to all appearance, "a people prepared for Lord". Many thousands of Christian people have been praying for Manchester, and hundreds of thousands of prayers have risen to God from Manchester herself for a blessing on the labours of His servants. The preparatory work, indeed, has been going on all the year, especially since the month of April, when united evangelistic services were held in almost all the nonconformist places of worship throughout the district. These preparatory meetings were brought to a close last Saturday, with a Communion service, in which upwards of 2,000 Christians of various denominations joined... There is no doubt that Messrs. Moody and Sankey have already made a most favourable impression upon a large portion of the Christian public of our city. The charm of Mr. Sankey's affectionate nature has been felt by many, as well as the power of his gift of song. The gifts which fit Mr. Moody to be the leader of a religious movement like the present are recognized by everyone."

"The crowds which flock to hear our friends, if they do not increase, continue undiminished. Already not a few have found peace in Jesus through their word. Mr. Moody has more than once said that nowhere, during the first week of his labours, have such meetings been held as in Manchester..."

"The first week of the meetings in Manchester has been full of good omen. The work of God for which we have so long prayed and waited has opened with power. God is bending in blessing over the city. An awakening and reviving breath from heaven has for some time been felt on the face of the churches. For months past, supplication has gone up to the throne from the noon and other prayer meetings in various parts of the city; and beheld, under the influence that swayed the churches have been gradually drawing closer together under the influence of the hope of revival."

"The clear exposition of God's way of salvation by faith, and not by works, illustrated and enforced by an admirable and telling use of Scripture and by graphic and pathetic story, wonderfully moved the great throng of men. Many shook with uncontrollable emotion, and much occasion for delightful labour was found in the inquiry-room. A man with whom the writer conversed, rose from his knees, where he had committed "his whole self" to Christ, and said, 'I came from Bolton today. I did not think I should find Christ!'"

"Afternoon meetings for women have been held in the Rev. A. McLaren's chapel, Oxford Road. It is strange to observe them thronging the road on their way to the chapel, and still more strange to see them occupying all the available to standing room in the spacious building. Not less than 2,000 women were present on Tuesday afternoon. These meetings, like all the rest, increase in power as they proceed, and on Thursday, when Mr. Moody entered the lecture hall, he found it filled with weeping, kneeling inquirers. Many left with the joy of pardon..."

"One feature of the noon meeting here is particularly striking, contrasted with what I have observed elsewhere, and that is the very large proportion of *men*, who, in this busy city (one of the busiest, I suppose in the world), leave their business to come and spend an hour in the middle of the day at the prayer-meeting. Another marked feature has been the spirit of prayer poured out on those who took part in the meetings. Is it not token for good when God is putting such deep, earnest longings for spiritual blessing into the hearts of His children, when the burden of every heart seems the same, and one yearning desire is heard in every petition for the revival of God's work in the hearts of His own people, and among the unsaved multitudes of this great city? I believe God is about to do a mighty work of grace in Manchester. Although but a few meetings have been held, we have had abundant proofs of the Lord's presence and power in the salvation of souls."

"The meeting in the Free Trade Hall last (Friday) night was the best I have seen here. The hall was crowded to excess, and the presence and power of God were most manifestly visible. It was one of the most solemn meetings I have ever attended, and at the close of the first meeting, when Mr. Moody announced that an inquiry-meeting would be held in the Oxford Hall, a large number went to that building, and the Christians present had the joy of pointing many anxious, seeking souls to the Lord Jesus."

The momentum was building...

"MANCHESTER, I REJOICE TO SAY, IS NOW ON FIRE. The most difficult of all English cities, perhaps, to be set on fire by anything but politics, is now fairly ablaze, and the flames are breaking out in all directions."

"Having referred to the case of a young man who had cried out in the inquiry-room on Friday night, "Oh, mother, I am coming!", the same young man sprang to his feet, and exclaimed in tones of impassioned earnestness, "THAT WAS ME!". The effect was electrical. Every eye was filled with tears. The whole vast assembly was impressed with a profound sense of the presence and power of the Holy Ghost."

"In bygone revivals such heart-smiting, conscience-stirring, soul-firing words as those which poured from the preacher's lips, would have caused hundreds to start to their feet, and cry out with frenzy, "God be merciful to me a sinner!" But in harmony with the prevailing character of this awakening, the conviction of sin produced on that occasion seemed to be too deep and too sacred to find expression in mere excited exclamations or physical prostrations, and were known only to Him who sees in secret! God was truly in the midst of us. The Holy Spirit came, as of old, with the force as of a rushing mighty wind, and filled all the place where we were sitting. The powers of the world to come were brought near to every conscience, in a manner never to be forgotten."

"Had Mr. Moody come to deliver only this one address, his mission had not been in vain. In the afternoon, from 15,000 to 17,000 struggled for admission. Various meetings had to be held in the Free Trade Hall, Oxford Hall, and Cavendish Chapel; all crowded as they never have been before. As many more halls of the same size could have been filled. From twenty to thirty meetings were held in the streets, where addresses were delivered by ministers and laymen. At every meeting the Lord was present to heal. Anxious inquirers were very numerous. Great numbers professed to find the Saviour."

"The meetings for Christian workers in the Free Trade Hall on Sunday mornings at eight o'clock have imparted a great stimulus to Christian labour. Never shall we forget Mr. Moody's address on "Daniel" last Sunday morning. The hall was crowded to excess; between 5,000 and 6,000 persons brought together at that early hour, in the depth of winter, testifies to the power with which the awakening has laid hold of the city."

"On Monday, Tuesday, and Wednesday there have been three meetings daily (at 12 noon, 3 afternoon, and 7:30 evening) in the Free Trade Hall, as well as the men's meetings, conducted by Mr. Drummond, in the Oxford Hall. Every night, scores of anxious inquirers have remained to be spoken with personally, and we very many have gone home from each meeting professing to have found peace and rest of soul by believing in the Lord Jesus Christ. The ministers and other Christian workers who have been engaged at these after-meetings in pointing seeking sinners to the Saviour, all testify that they have never seen such a wonderful work of grace in this city. This work is not only seen in the large numbers of the unconverted, but also in the revival and refreshing of the children of God and the uniting together different sections of the Church of Christ in the common goal of seeking the salvation of perishing souls... Several meetings of the clergy and ministers of all denominations have been held with the object of promoting this Christian union and carrying on the blessed work after Mr. Moody and Mr.

Sankey have left."

"On the [final] Thursday morning, Mr. Moody addressed a crowded meeting in Higher Broughton Presbyterian Church, and then came on to the noon prayer meeting in the Oxford Hall, where he read and commented on the earlier part of the 103rd Psalm. He said he had to bless the Lord for what He had done for him. It had been the best year of his life. He had been more used by God than in all the seventeen preceding years." He was clearly delighted with the results of the Manchester campaign.

No numbers added to the church in Manchester in the 1874 revival are given in these reports, although it is safe to say that, based on numbers in other cities (such as Glasgow), at least 5,000 people were added. These figures would not have included the previously nominal Christians who were already part of an established church. Then the renewing effect on the churches also needs to be taken into consideration, with many thousands strengthened in their faith and encouraged in their witness. Indeed, one after-effect of the visit of Moody and Sankey was a visitation of every home in Manchester and Salford: "By a special arrangement, as it seemed, of Providence, Mr. Reginald Radcliffe was present, and immediately put before them a definite plan for making a great gospel attack upon the city. He suggested that an ordinance map of Manchester should be cut into small squares, each representing a district, and that two or three young persons should undertake to carry the gospel, in the shape of a tract or otherwise, to every house, great and small, within that district, so that no single dwelling should be omitted."

On one side of these tracts was printed the hymn "Jesus of Nazareth passeth by" (Appendix 1E) and on the other, a short address by Mr. Moody, his text being Revelation 3:20:

"Behold, I stand at the door and knock : if any man hear my voice and open the door, I will come in to him, and sup with him, and he with Me" (Rev. iii. 20). A woman in Glasgow got into difficulties. Her rent was due, but she had no money for the landlord, and she knew very well that he would turn her out if she did not satisfy his claim. In despair, she knew not what to do. A Christian man heard of her distress, and came to her door with money to help her. He knocked, but although he thought he could hear someone inside, yet the door was not opened. He knocked again, but still there was no response. The third time he knocked, but that door still remained locked and barred against him! Some time after he met this woman in the streets, and told her how he had gone to her house to pay her rent, but could not get in. 'Oh, sir!' she exclaimed, was that you? Why, I thought it was the landlord, and I was afraid to open the door!'

Dear friends! Christ is knocking at the door of your heart. He has knocked many times already, and now He knocks again by this message. He is your best Friend, although, like that woman, perhaps, you think He comes with the stern voice of justice to demand the payment of your great sin-debt. If so, you are sadly mistaken. He comes not to *demand*, but to *give*!' He knows you can never pay the great debt you owe to God. He knows that, if that debt is not paid for you, you are forever lost! He loves you, though He hates your sins; and, in order that you might be saved, laid down His life as a sacrifice for the guilty. And, now, He comes! bringing the gift of salvation to the door of your hearts. *Will you receive the gift?* D. L. Moody." [54]

Moody and Sankey left Manchester on the last day of 1874 and went on to hold great campaigns in Sheffield, Birmingham, Liverpool and London. They published a hymn book "Sacred Songs and Solos", which became very popular nationwide. The work in Manchester appears to have continued strongly into 1875.

On the 3rd of August, 1875, a great farewell meeting for Moody and Sankey was held in Liverpool. In his closing speech, Moody said "I hope there will be a fresh interest awakened in Liverpool as there has been in Manchester. I do not know of anything that has encouraged me more than to hear of the work going on in Manchester for the last six weeks. I hope Liverpool and Manchester will shake hands in carrying on the work…God bless you, and may the power of God come upon you this morning afresh". [55].

7 A FAREWELL TO HENRY MOORHOUSE: MANCHESTER'S GREATEST EVANGELIST

Taken mainly from "Chief Men Among the Brethren" by Henry Pickering

During the last few years of his life Henry found work similar to that of his early days in preaching and selling Scriptures from a horse-drawn Bible carriage. In two years he sold over 150,000 Bibles and Testaments, and gave away millions of books and tracts. Sadly, his health was deteriorating and he no longer had strength to preach to the crowds.

In 1876 his service was evidently closing, his last year of labour was one of much suffering, the doctors said his heart was twice the size it ought to be, yet he was ever bright and happy. Near the end he said, "If it were the Lord's will to raise me up again, I should like to preach more on the text 'God so loved the world'." On 28th December, 1880, in his fortieth year, he passed Home to receive the "Well done," and to enter into "the joy of his Lord."

The two veterans, Richard Weaver and Henry

Moorhouse, lie not far from each other in Ardwick Cemetery, Manchester. John 3:16 is engraved on the memorial to Moorhouse. Note: this Cemetery closed in 1950 and is no longer visible, but Henry's gravestone (pictured below) was saved and now lies at Inskip Baptist Church, near Preston. [56]

John Hambleton, in relating his farewell interview with Henry, aptly summed up his life: "Calling to see him on Monday last, before he left us, I grasped his arms, as his face betokened that the enemy death was doing his last work, and said, 'Harry, we shall soon meet up yonder.' He replied, while gasping for breath, 'Sure, sure, sure, it's all sure and well'. [57] How plainly visible is the work of God in putting into such a little frail vessel as our brother such a treasure, showing us all that 'the excellency of the power is of God' [2 Corinthians 4:7]."

Henry's last letter aptly summed up his own life. "Ask prayer for me to suffer for Christ better than ever I preached for Him; I ONLY WANT TO GLORIFY HIM." [58]

Henry Moorhouse's contribution to the revivals in Manchester (and elsewhere) was incalculable. In my opinion, he deserves to be remembered with the accolade "Manchester's greatest evangelist".

In Loving Memory
of
HENRY MOORHOUSE
MARY
WIFE OF THE ABOVE
WE HAVE LOVED
WE LOVE WE SHALL LOVE

ENDNOTES

1. https://manchestermethodists.org.uk/about/history/.

2. H. Rack "Between Church and Sect: The Origins of Methodism in Manchester" https://www.escholar.manchester.ac.uk/api/datastream?publicationPid=uk-ac-man-scw:1m4004&datastreamId=POST-PEER-REVIEW-PUBLISHERS-DOCUMENT.PDF

3.https://www.dmbi.online/index.php?do=app.entry&id=1804

4. https://www.revival-library.org/revival_heroes/19th_century/caughey_james.shtml

5. "Recollections of Reginald Radcliffe" by his wife. https://archive.org/stream/recollectionsofr00radc/recollectionsofr00radc_djvu.txt

6. https://www.1859.org.uk/the-people-god-used/john-hambleton.

7. M. Backholer "Global Revival - Worldwide Outpourings, Forty-three Visitations of the Holy Spirit: The Great Commission - Revivals in Asia, Africa, Europe, North & South America, Australia and Oceania".

8. Selwyn Hughes. Quoted in M. Backholer "Global

Revival"

9. https://www.geoffgreen.org.uk/uk-revivals

10. "Recollections of Reginald Radcliffe"

11. G. Green https://www.liverpoolrevival.org.uk/other-revivals/1859-revival

12. J. E. Orr "The Second Evangelical Awakening. An Account of the Second Worldwide Evangelical Revival Beginning in the Mid-Nineteenth Century" published 1949.

13. M. Marcel https://ukwells.org/revivalists/revival-in-england-1859-1865

14. J. MacPherson "Henry Moorhouse: The English Evangelist"
https://archive.org/stream/henrymoorhouseen00macp/henrymoorhouseen00macp_djvu.txt

15. Quoted in https://ukwells.org/revivalists/revival-in-england-1859-1865

16.https://en.wikipedia.org/wiki/Charles_Grandison_Finney

17. http://daibach-welldigger.blogspot.com/2017/03/charles-finney-and-wales.html.

18. https://www.1859.org.uk/the-people-god-used/reginald-radcliffe

19. https://www.1859.org.uk/the-people-god-used/richard-weaver-national

20. https://bibletruthpublishers.com/harrison-ord/henry-pickering/chief-men-among-the-brethren/hy-pickering/la129704

21. https://www.1859.org.uk/the-people-god-used/henry-moorhouse.

22. J. MacPherson "Henry Moorhouse: The English Evangelist".

23.https://www.rogercarswell.net/articles/2019/11/1/henry-moorhouse-gravestone

24. John Rylands was a wealthy Manchester merchant. There is a famous library named after him in Deansgate (now part of the University of Manchester).

25. https://www.1859.org.uk/the-people-god-used/henry-moorhouse.

26. J. Hambleton "Buds, Blossoms, and Fruits of the Revival. A testimony to the great work of God in these last days".
https://www.brethrenarchive.org/people/john-hambleton/pamphlets/buds-blossoms-and-fruits-of-the-revival/

27. http://uplook.org/1999/05/john-hambleton/

28.https://www.brethrenarchive.org/media/358253/benn

ett-e-h-_-the-converted-actor-john-hambleton.pdf

29. Henry Pickering "Chief men among the brethren" https://bibletruthpublishers.com/john-hambleton/henry-pickering/chief-men-among-the-brethren/hy-pickering/la129676

30. C. G. Finney https://www.gospeltruth.net/memoirsrestored/memrest35.htm

31.https://www.gospeltruth.net/memoirsrestored/memrest35.htm

32. https://ukwells.org/wells/manchester-corn-exchange

33. https://ukwells.org/wells/free-trade-hall-manchester

34. James Caughey taught the doctrine of entire sanctification as a secondary experience to salvation (justification), as did John Wesley.

35. https://ukwells.org/wells/james-caughey-rochdale-meeting

36. https://ukwells.org/wells/rochdale-2

37. https://ukwells.org/wells/presbyterian-free-church-salford

38. https://www.brethrenarchive.org/people/john-hambleton/pamphlets/buds-blossoms-and-fruits-of-the-revival/

39. as 38.

40. https://ukwells.org/wells/chalmers-presbyterian-church-ancoats

41. https://ukwells.org/wells/harpurhey-union-chapel

42. https://ukwells.org/wells/duckinfield

43. https://ukwells.org/wells/cockerhill

44. https://ukwells.org/wells/smithfield-market-manchester

45. https://ukwells.org/wells/alhambra-circus-manchester

46. https://www.liverpoolrevival.org.uk/other-revivals

47.https://www.christianitytoday.com/history/people/evangelistsandapologists/dwight-l-moody.html

48. E. Elliott "The man who moved the man who moved the world." 2016.
https://medium.com/@edelliott/the-man-who-moved-the-man-who-moved-the-world-e5a802940bd1

49. https://bibletruthpublishers.com/henry-moorhouse/henry-pickering/chief-men-among-the-brethren/hy-pickering/print-friendly/lxpf-la-129705

50. "Henry Moorhouse: The English Evangelist" p86

51. F. C. Bailey "D.L. Moody: The Greatest Evangelist of the Nineteenth Century" Moody Publishers, 1937

52. https://www.biblestudytools.com/classics/moody-gospel-awakening/moody-and-sankey-in-great-britain.html

53. "Narrative of Messrs. Moody and Sankey's Labors in Scotland and Ireland. Also, in Manchester, Sheffield and Birmingham, England." ANSON D. F. RANDOLPH & COMPANY, 770 BROADWAY, COR. 9th STREET, NEW YORK, 1875. Author Unknown. https://play.google.com/books/reader?id=rjRGAAAAYAAJ&pg=GBS.PA102&hl=en

54. As 53

55. E. J. Goodspeed and I. E. Sankey "A Full History of the Wonderful Career of Moody and Sankey in Great Britain and America." 1876 https://www.google.co.uk/books/edition/A_Full_History_of_the_Wonderful_Career_o/6av3YJ8-KBcC?hl=en&gbpv=1

56.https://www.rogercarswell.net/articles/2019/11/1/henry-moorhouse-gravestone

57. "Henry Moorhouse: The English Evangelist" p138

58. H. Pickering "Chief Men Among the Brethren" https://bibletruthpublishers.com/henry-moorhouse/henry-pickering/chief-men-among-the-brethren/hy-pickering/la129705

IMAGES

Front cover image: Ancoats ca. 1870. https://elizabethgaskellhouse.co.uk/elizabeth-gaskells-home-in-hampshire-part-1/ancoats-c-1870-c-manchester-libraries/

Henry Moorhouse: https://www.evangelical-times.org/wp-content/uploads/2018/07/Henry-Moorhouse.jpg

Henry Moorhouse Gravestone: https://www.rogercarswell.net/articles/2019/11/1/henry-moorhouse-gravestone

Appendix 1: Hymns sung during the Revival

A. O happy day that fixed my choice

1 O happy day that fixed my choice
On Thee, my Saviour and my God!
Well may this glowing heart rejoice,
And tell its raptures all abroad.

Refrain:
Happy day, happy day,
When Jesus washed my sins away!
He taught me how to watch and pray,
And live rejoicing every day;
Happy day, happy day,
When Jesus washed my sins away!

2 O happy bond, that seals my vows
To Him who merits all my love!
Let cheerful anthems fill His house,
While to that sacred shrine I move. [Refrain]

3 'Tis done, the great transaction's done;
I am my Lord's and He is mine;
He drew me and I followed on,
Rejoiced to own the call divine. [Refrain]

4 Now rest, my long-divided heart,
Fixed on this blissful centre, rest;
Here have I found a nobler part,
Here heavenly pleasures fill my breast. [Refrain]

5 High heaven that hears the solemn vow,
That vow renewed shall daily hear;

Till in life's latest hour I bow,
And bless, in death, a bond so dear. [Refrain]

Philip Doddridge (1702-1751)

An example of the hymns sung at the time of the 1859-62 revival
https://hymnary.org/text/o_happy_day_that_fixed_my_choice

B. My Heart is Fixed, Eternal God (Christ for me)

1
My heart is fixed, eternal God,
Fixed on Thee, fixed on Thee;
And my immortal choice is made,
Christ for me, Christ for me.
He is the Prophet, Priest and King,
Who did for me salvation bring;
And while I live I mean to sing,
Christ for me, Christ for me.

2
In Him I see the Godhead shine,
Christ for me, Christ for me;
He is the Majesty divine,
Christ for me, Christ for me.
The Father's well-belovèd Son,
Co-partner of His royal throne,
Who did for human guilt atone,
Christ for me, Christ for me.

3
Let others boast of heaps of gold,
Christ for me, Christ for me;
His riches never can be told,
Christ for me, Christ for me.

Your gold will waste and wear away,
Your honors perish in a day;
My portion never can decay,
Christ for me, Christ for me.

4

In pining sickness, or in health,
Christ for me, Christ for me;
In deepest poverty or wealth,
Christ for me, Christ for me.
And in that all-important day
When I the summons shall obey,
And pass from this dark world away,
Christ for me, Christ for me.

5

At home, abroad, by night and day,
Christ for me, Christ for me;
Where'er I speak, or sing, or pray;
Christ for me, Christ for me.
Him first, Him last, Him all day long,
My hope, my solace and my song;
He sweetly leads my soul along,
Christ for me, Christ for me.

Richard Jukes (1804-67)
https://bibletruthpublishers.com/my-heart-is-fixed-eternal-God/echoes-of-grace-hymnbook-243/lkh243EGHB

C. I hear Thy Welcome Voice

1

I hear Thy welcome voice,
That calls me, Lord, to Thee,
For cleansing in Thy precious blood
That flowed on Calvary.

Chorus
I am coming, Lord,
Coming now to Thee:
Wash me, cleanse me in the blood
That flowed on Calvary.
2
Though coming weak and vile,
Thou dost my strength assure;
Thou dost my vileness fully cleanse,
Till spotless all, and pure.
3
'Tis Jesus who confirms
The blessed work within,
By adding grace to welcomed grace,
Where reigned the power of sin.
4
And He the witness gives
To loyal hearts and free,
That every promise is fulfilled,
If faith but brings the plea.
5
All hail, redeeming blood!
All hail, life-giving grace!
All hail, the gift of Christ our Lord,
Our strength and righteousness.

Lewis Hartsough (1828-1919)
https://www.hymnal.net/en/hymn/h/1051
An example of the hymns used in Moody/Sankey campaigns

D. There is a Fountain

1. There is a fountain filled with blood
Drawn from Immanuel's veins;
And sinners, plunged beneath that flood,
Lose all their guilty stains:
Lose all their guilty stains,
Lose all their guilty stains;
And sinners, plunged beneath that flood,
Lose all their guilty stains.

2. The dying thief rejoiced to see
That fountain in his day;
And there may I, though vile as he,
Wash all my sins away:
Wash all my sins away,
Wash all my sins away;
And there may I, though vile as he,
Wash all my sins away.

3. Dear dying Lamb, Thy precious blood
Shall never lose its power,
Till all the ransomed ones of God
Be saved, to sin no more:
Be saved, to sin no more,
Be saved, to sin no more;
Till all the ransomed ones of God,
Be saved to sin no more.

4. E'er since by faith I saw the stream
Thy flowing wounds supply,
Redeeming love has been my theme,
And shall be till I die:
And shall be till I die,

And shall be till I die;
Redeeming love has been my theme,
And shall be till I die.

5. When this poor lisping, stammering tongue
Lies silent in the grave,
Then in a nobler, sweeter song,
I'll sing Thy power to save:
I'll şing Thy power to save,
I'll sing Thy power to save;
Then in a nobler, sweeter song,
I'll sing Thy power to save.

William Cowper (1731-1800)
https://www.hymnal.net/en/hymn/h/1006
An example of the hymns used in Moody/Sankey campaigns.

E. Jesus of Nazareth passeth by

1. What means this eager, anxious throng,
Which moves with busy haste along,
These wondrous gath'rings day by day?
What means this strange commotion, say?
In accents hushed the throng reply:
"Jesus of Nazareth passeth by."
In accents hushed the throng reply:
"Jesus of Nazareth passeth by."

Refrain:
Passeth by, passeth by,
Jesus of Nazareth passeth by.
Passeth by, passeth by,
Jesus of Nazareth passeth by.

2. Who is this Jesus? Why should He
The city move so mightily?
A passing stranger, has He skill
To move the multitude at will?
Again the stirring tones reply:
"Jesus of Nazareth passeth by."
Again the stirring tones reply:
"Jesus of Nazareth passeth by."

3. Jesus! 'tis He who once below
Man's pathway trod, 'mid pain and woe;
And burdened ones, where'er He came,
Bro't out their sick and deaf and lame.
The blind rejoiced to hear the cry:
"Jesus of Nazareth passeth by."
The blind rejoiced to hear the cry:
"Jesus of Nazareth passeth by?"

4. Again He comes! from place to place
His holy footprints we can trace.
He pauseth at our threshold, nay,
He enters,– condescends to stay.
Shall we not gladly raise the cry:
"Jesus of Nazareth passeth by?"
Shall we not gladly raise the cry
"Jesus of Nazareth passeth by?"

5. Ho! all ye heavy laden, come!
Here's pardon, comfort, rest and home.
Ye wand'rers from a Father's face,
Return, accept His proffered grace,
Ye tempted, there's a refuge nigh:
"Jesus of Nazareth passeth by."

Ye tempted, there's a refuge nigh:
"Jesus of Nazareth passeth by."

6. But if you still this call refuse,
And all his wond'rous love abuse,
Soon will He sadly from you turn,
Your bitter pray'r for pardon spurn.
"Too late! too late!" will be the cry:
"Jesus of Nazareth has passed by."
"Too late! too late!" will be the cry:
"Jesus of Nazareth has passed by."

Has passed by, has passed by,
Jesus of Nazareth has passed by.
Has passed by, has passed by,
Jesus of Nazareth has passed by.

Emma F. R. Campbell (1830-1919)
Source: His Fullness Songs #349
https://hymnary.org/text/what_means_this_eager_anxious_throng

AFTERWORD

"History tells us that revivals often start when people read about past revivals". If this book has provoked you to pray and work to see another revival, why not share this book with a friend?

I would like to write about other times of renewal/revival in Manchester. If you have stories or other information you can contact me at apaulmould@hotmail.co.uk. I am especially interested in testimonies from the time of the Toronto Blessing (1994-95).

ABOUT THE AUTHOR

Paul was born in Leicestershire, England, but has spent almost all his adult life in the Manchester area. He formerly worked as a Biochemist, Cell Biologist, and Biophysicist at the University of Manchester, UK. Following his recent retirement he has acted as a Trustee of a local Foodbank, led a bible study for refugees, and taken up his enthusiasm for Christian writing. This is his fourth book, which has been on his heart to write for several years. Paul loves to read about past revivals but his special interest is the Person and work of the Holy Spirit.

Previous Books by the Author:

Mould, Paul "Secure Foundations: An Introductory Course for New Christians", Kindle Edition 2021. https://www.amazon.co.uk/Secure-Foundations-Introductory-Christians-Christian-ebook/dp/B08V4P48P8/ref=sr_1_1?dchild=1&keywords=Paul+mould&qid=1631349512&s=digital-text&sr=1-1

Mould, Paul "The Hope of Glory: The Wonderful Future Promised to Christians" Kindle Edition 2021. https://www.amazon.co.uk/Hope-Glory-Wonderful-Christians-Foundations-ebook/dp/B094LD5HML/ref=sr_1_2?dchild=1&keywords=paul+mould&qid=1631347029&s=digital-text&sr=1-2

Mould, Paul. "Honouring the Holy Spirit". Kindle Edition 2021. https://www.amazon.co.uk/Honouring-Holy-Spirit-Paul-Mould-ebook/dp/B09G3BTPDF/ref=sr_1_1?keywords=paul+mould&qid=1637006470&s=digital-text&sr=1-1

Mould, Paul. "Honouring the Holy Spirit". Paperback Edition 2021. Amazon Publishing ISBN: 9798479238550. https://www.amazon.co.uk/Honouring-Holy-Spirit-Paul-Mould/dp/B09GJG6X85/ref=tmm_pap_swatch_0?_encoding=UTF8&qid=1637006470&sr=1-1

Printed in Great Britain
by Amazon

70403815R00058